my revision notes

Edexcel AS/A-level History

BRITAIN 1625–1701

CONFLICT, REVOLUTION AND SETTLEMENT

David Farr

Series editor
Peter Callaghan

HODDER
EDUCATION
AN HACHETTE UK COMPANY

Acknowledgements

The Publishers would like to thank the following for permission to reproduce copyright material.

p.75 and **p.81** from B. Coward, *The Stuart Age* (1980), Copyright © Taylor and Francis Group. Reproduced by permission of Taylor & Francis Books UK **p.75**, **p.77**, **p.81** from J. Miller, *The Glorious Revolution* (1983), Copyright © Taylor and Francis Group. Reproduced by permission of Taylor & Francis Books UK **p.79** and **p.85** reproduced with permission of John Wiley & Sons, Inc., from D.L. Smith, *A History of the Modern British Isles, 1603–1707* (1998), permission conveyed through Copyright Clearance Center, Inc.

Every effort has been made to trace all copyright holders, but if any have been inadvertently overlooked, the Publishers will be pleased to make the necessary arrangements at the first opportunity.

Although every effort has been made to ensure that website addresses are correct at time of going to press, Hodder Education cannot be held responsible for the content of any website mentioned in this book. It is sometimes possible to find a relocated web page by typing in the address of the home page for a website in the URL window of your browser.

Hachette UK's policy is to use papers that are natural, renewable and recyclable products and made from wood grown in sustainable forests. The logging and manufacturing processes are expected to conform to the environmental regulations of the country of origin.

Orders: please contact Bookpoint Ltd, 130 Milton Park, Abingdon, Oxon OX14 4SE. Telephone: +44 (0)1235 827720. Fax: +44 (0)1235 400454. Email education@bookpoint.co.uk Lines are open from 9 a.m. to 5 p.m., Monday to Saturday, with a 24-hour message answering service. You can also order through our website: www.hoddereducation.co.uk

ISBN: 978 1 4718 7655 4

© David Farr 2017

First published in 2017 by

Hodder Education,

An Hachette UK Company

Carmelite House

50 Victoria Embankment

London EC4Y 0DZ

www.hoddereducation.co.uk

Impression number   10 9 8 7 6 5 4 3 2 1

Year   2020   2019   2018   2017

Cover photo © Jozef Sedmak/Alamy Stock Photo
Illustrations by Integra
Typeset by Integra Software Services Pvt. Ltd., Pondicherry, India
Printed in Spain

A catalogue record for this title is available from the British Library.

My revision planner

Historical interpretations: How revolutionary, in the years to 1701, was the Glorious Revolution of 1688–89?

Introduction

About Paper 1

Paper 1 Option 1C: Britain, 1625–1701: Conflict, revolution and settlement requires a breadth of knowledge of a historical period, as well as a knowledge of the historical debate around the Glorious Revolution. Paper 1 tests you against two Assessment Objectives: AO1 and AO3.

AO1 tests your ability to:
● organise and communicate your own knowledge
● analyse and evaluate key features of the past
● make supported judgements
● deal with concepts of cause, consequence, change, continuity, similarity, difference and significance.

In Paper 1, AO1 tasks require you to write essays from your own knowledge.

AO3 tests your ability to:
● analyse and evaluate interpretations of the past
● explore interpretations of the past in the context of historical debate.

In Paper 1, the AO3 task requires you to write an essay which analyses the work of historians.

At A-level, Paper 1 is worth 30 per cent of your qualification. At AS-level, Paper 1 is worth 60 per cent of your qualification.

The exam

The Paper 1 AS and A-level exam lasts for 2 hours and 15 minutes, and is divided into three sections.

Section A and Section B test the breadth of your historical knowledge of the four themes:
● Section A requires you to write one essay from a choice of two. Section A questions will usually test your knowledge of at least a decade. You should spend around 35 to 40 minutes on Section A – this includes making a brief plan.
● Section B requires you to write one essay from a choice of two. Section B essays usually test your knowledge of a third of the period 1625–88, around 23 years. You should spend around 35 to 40 minutes on Section B – this includes making a brief plan.

Section C tests your knowledge of the debate around the revolutionary nature of the Glorious Revolution.

● Section C requires you to answer one compulsory question relating to two extracts from the work of historians. Questions will focus on the years 1688–1701. You should spend around 35 to 40 minutes on Section C, and an additional 20 minutes to read the sources and make a plan.

The AS questions are of a lower level of demand in order to differentiate them from the A-level questions. You will find examples of AS and A-level questions throughout the book.

How to use this book

This book has been designed to help you to develop the knowledge and skills necessary to succeed in this exam.
● The book is divided into five sections – one for each of the Themes in Depth, and one for the Historical Interpretation.
● Each section is made up of a series of topics organised into double-page spreads.
● On the left-hand page, you will find a summary of the key content you need to learn.
● Words in bold in the key content are defined in the glossary.
● On the right-hand page, you will find exam-focused activities.

Together, these two strands of the book will take you through the knowledge and skills essential for exam success.

Examination activities

There are three levels of exam-focused activities.
● Band 1 activities are designed to develop the foundational skills needed to pass the exam. These have a green heading and this symbol.
● Band 2 activities are designed to build on the skills developed in Band 1 activities and to help you achieve a C grade. These have an orange heading and this symbol.
● Band 3 activities are designed to enable you to access the highest grades. These have a purple heading and this symbol.

Some of the activities have answers or suggested answers on pages 96–8. These have the following symbol to indicate this.

Each section ends with an exam-style question and model high-level answer with commentary. This should give you guidance on what is required to achieve the top grades.

1 The quest for political stability, 1625–88

Charles I and parliament, 1625–29

In the period 1625–29 Charles I called three parliaments in order to secure finance for his foreign policy. Three parliaments in such a short period indicates that Charles' relationship with parliament had rapidly deteriorated. Trust broke down over the interrelated issues of religion, foreign policy, finance and problems of government.

Religion

Charles' religious policy created political tension. The king's open support for **Arminianism**, a form of Protestantism, alienated the majority of the political class – those who had economic, social and political influence. Many viewed Arminianism as being dangerously close to **Catholicism**. Charles' support for Arminianism was shown through:

- promoting the Arminian **Richard Montagu** to his royal chaplain in the face of parliamentary calls for Montagu's **impeachment** (1625)
- allowing his **favourite**, the **Duke of Buckingham**, to state his favour for Arminianism at the York House Conference (1626)
- making the Arminian **William Laud** the Bishop of London (1628).

Foreign policy

Charles' foreign policy was a failure. In 1625 he called parliament to fund an attack on the Spanish, but the raid on Cadiz was a disaster. When Charles sought to help the Protestant French **Huguenots**, his forces were again defeated at La Rochelle in 1627. Both of these defeats were regarded as national humiliations. Parliament's anger was directed against the king's favourite, the Duke of Buckingham, who had overseen foreign policy. Parliament wanted him impeached – however, Charles refused to sacrifice Buckingham as a scapegoat. The assassination of Buckingham in 1628, and the public rejoicing at his death, merely increased Charles' hostility towards parliament.

Finance

In order to finance foreign policy Charles needed to raise additional income through taxation, which needed parliamentary approval. In 1625 parliament agreed to two **subsidies** amounting to £140,000. This fell well short of the £1 million Charles needed, so he asked the Commons for more. Parliament refused and in 1626,

when short of funds, Charles dissolved parliament and sought other means of raising income. He levied a **forced loan** worth five subsidies, which was taxation that had not been agreed by parliament. Although the loan was successful in raising money, it caused a significant amount of resentment.

Five knights who refused to pay were imprisoned and refused bail – this became known as the Five Knights' case. For many, this was a clear indication of Charles' **absolutist** intentions – the king was not only taxing without consent, but also imprisoning as he wished.

Problems of government: the Petition of Right, 1628

Charles' policies in religion, foreign policy and finance led many MPs to assert that the king was acting illegally and contrary to the established forms of government. When Charles called his third parliament in 1628 he demanded the immediate granting of taxes to continue the wars. However, MPs decided that no money would be granted unless their various grievances were addressed. Parliament presented their grievances in the Petition of Right:

- There should be no taxation without the consent of parliament.
- There should be no imprisonment without cause shown.
- There should be no **billeting** of soldiers or sailors upon householders against their will.
- There should be no **martial law** to punish ordinary offences by sailors or soldiers.

Desperate for parliamentary funds, the king accepted the Petition on 7 June 1628, but his written reply did not use the traditional form of words and thus denied the Petition lawful status. The Commons insisted on the correct response and Charles eventually gave it.

Charles' reaction to the Petition forced MPs to make a more direct statement of their concerns with the Three Resolutions of 2 March 1629. These denounced Arminianism and encouraged merchants to refuse to pay **tonnage and poundage**.

On 10 March 1629 Charles announced the dissolution of parliament. He resolved to govern without parliament, and embarked upon eleven years of Personal Rule.

Spot the mistake a

Below are a sample exam question and a paragraph written in answer to this question. Why does this paragraph not get into Level 4? Once you have identified the mistake, rewrite the paragraph so that it displays the qualities of Level 4.

> How accurate is it to say that religion was the main cause for the deterioration in the relationship between Charles I and parliament in the years 1625 to 1637?

Religion was an important issue in undermining the relationship between Charles I and parliament in the years 1625 to 1637. From 1625 Charles sought to impose Arminianism as his favoured approach. In doing so he alienated the majority of the political class. In 1625 Charles supported Montagu against parliament. In 1626 Charles personally made his position clear at the York House Conference. In 1628 he promoted William Laud. In all of these things he did not seek any compromise but believed he had the right, as Supreme Governor of the Church, to do what he wanted in religious policy. After 1629 Charles continued to impose Arminianism.

 Mind map

Use the information on the opposite page to add detail to the mind map below about the deteriorating relationship between Charles I and parliament.

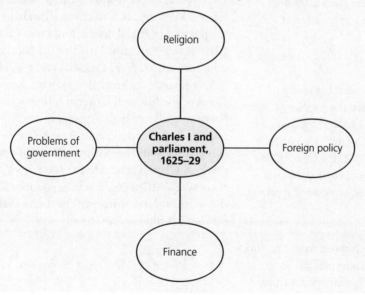

Personal Rule and its failure, 1629–40

The Personal Rule was the period of eleven years when Charles I governed without parliament. It came to an end after events in Scotland forced Charles to recall parliament in 1640.

Finance

Charles sought to secure his financial position so that he would not have to recall parliament. Peace with France in 1629 and Spain in 1630 enabled him to reduce his major costs. The king exploited traditional feudal dues, payments which the crown controlled and which did not need parliamentary approval. For example, monopolies were granted to individuals or groups of merchants who had exclusive rights to import a product and fix its price at a high level.

The key source of income for Charles was **Ship Money**. Traditionally, this was levied only on coastal counties for defence purposes, but in 1635 it was extended as a national tax and continued until 1640. Ship Money proved very successful. At a time when a parliamentary subsidy was worth about £70,000, Ship Money alone gave Charles an average of £200,000 annually making it less likely that he would have to recall parliament to secure further funds. However, methods of assessing and collecting the tax caused much opposition and resentment.

Hampden's Case

In October 1637 John Hampden, a member of the Buckinghamshire **gentry**, challenged the legality of Ship Money and refused to pay the tax. His trial became a test case on the legality of Ship Money, which was upheld by seven of the 12 judges hearing the case. Public opinion was alarmed by the verdict, which confirmed that the king could raise taxation without parliamentary approval.

Religion

In the 1630s Charles continued to impose Arminianism through William Laud, who was appointed as Archbishop of Canterbury in 1633. The key measures of **Laudianism** focused on the so-called 'beauty of holiness', through the wearing of **vestments** and the use of music, candles and altar cloths. To ensure conformity, these measures were enforced through the use of **visitations** and supervision through the church courts. For visitations, bishops' representatives reported which churches were conforming and brought any offenders before church courts.

Opposition

Initially, there was little opposition to Laudianism. Those who opposed its imposition were a minority, predominantly the more radical **Puritans** whose strength of belief made some of them more inclined to protest. The limited examples of open opposition indicate that there was general passive acceptance of Laudianism.

Scotland

In 1637 Charles decided to impose the Laudian Prayer Book on Presbyterian Scotland, without consulting the Scottish parliament. Widespread rioting broke out and in 1638 many nobles and clergy signed the **National Covenant**, swearing to resist all changes to the **Scottish Kirk**. The military conflicts which followed, known as the **Bishops' War**, were inconclusive: the Scots were well organised and motivated, whereas Charles had insufficient funds to pay for his military campaigns.

The collapse of Personal Rule

In 1640 Charles called a parliament to finance an army to crush the Scots. This 'Short Parliament' only lasted three weeks before it was dissolved by Charles who refused MPs' demands to remove Laudianism and end the practice of feudal dues before they would grant funds. Charles was determined to force the Scots to comply without parliamentary financial backing. However, this lack of finance undermined his attack against the Scottish forces of the National Covenant. In August 1640 the Scots invaded northern England and occupied Newcastle. Charles was forced to negotiate with the Scots and agreed they could keep Newcastle until a settlement was reached. Charles agreed to pay the Scots £850 a day until there was a settlement, and in September 1640 writs went out to summon parliament. The 'Long Parliament' met for the first time in November.

ⓘ Complete the paragraph ⓐ

Below are a sample exam question and a paragraph written in answer to this question. The paragraph contains a point and specific examples, but lacks a concluding analytical link back to the question. Complete the paragraph, adding this link in the space provided.

How far did the system of feudal dues improve Charles I's financial position in the years 1629 to 1640?

> After dissolving parliament in 1629 Charles was determined not to recall parliament again. To achieve this, he needed to improve his financial position, so he used his prerogative and the collection of traditional feudal dues. Some of Charles' measures included…
>
> _____
>
> _____

ⓘ Delete as applicable ⓐ

Below are a sample exam question and a paragraph written in answer to this question. Read the paragraph and decide which of the possible options (in bold) is most appropriate. Delete the least appropriate options and complete the paragraph by justifying your selection.

How far did the imposition of Laudianism undermine Charles' government in the years 1628 to 1640?

> Charles I's imposition of Laudianism undermined his government to a **great/fair/ limited** extent. For example, the 'beauty of holiness', which involved the introduction and enforcement of the use of more visual forms of religion, was unpopular with Puritans. This involved the use of vestments and music as part of services. Laudianism was enforced through the use of visitations and church courts. Charles I's imposition did not undermine his government, as the visual aspects of Laudianism were **extremely/ moderately/slightly** successful…
>
> _____
>
> _____

Division and the drift towards civil war

In 1640 most MPs were united against what they regarded as the abuses of Charles' Personal Rule. They agreed to abolish Ship Money and passed a Triennial Act, which meant that the monarch would have to call a parliament at least every three years. Charles would therefore not be able to repeat an extended period of Personal Rule. However, divisions among MPs began to emerge over the following areas:

● Root and Branch Petition, December 1640: This petition, from 15,000 London Puritans and supported by the radical MP **John Pym,** called for the removal of bishops from the church. Conservatives viewed this as a threat to the established order.
● Bill of Attainder, May 1641: This was used in parliament by Pym to justify the execution of Charles' principal minister, Thomas Wentworth, Earl of Stafford. A Bill of Attainder needed less evidence to convict someone if they were regarded as a threat to the state. Conservatives worried that using such a device was bending the law in a way that was as much a threat to the **constitution** as Charles' actions.
● Militia Bill, November 1641: This bill proposed that parliament should control any army used to crush the Irish Rebellion that began in October 1641. Conservatives regarded this as a direct threat to the most important royal **prerogative** – command of the armed forces.
● Grand Remonstrance, November 1641: Pym, in order to persuade wavering MPs to pass the Militia Bill, produced the Grand Remonstrance, a document listing Charles' faults since 1625 and thus reasons why he could not be trusted with armed forces. The moderates in the Commons saw little point in dragging up old grievances which had been resolved by legislation already passed. They also disliked the way the Remonstrance was not addressed to the king but seemed to be an appeal to the people.

Most moderate MPs regarded these as examples of increasing, and dangerous, radicalism. The reaction to Pym and his supporters became known as **constitutional royalism**, a number of moderates prepared to support royalism as a source of order and stability. This helped to create the two sides necessary for civil war.

The coming of the Civil War, January–August 1642

In January 1642 Charles tried to arrest his five leading parliamentary opponents, accusing them of seeking to subvert the laws and government of England and encouraging the Scots to invade England. The 'Five Members' had been forewarned and fled. The attempt to arrest the Five Members proved the final straw for the parliamentary opposition and highlighted how the king could no longer be trusted and that he was determined to restore his authority by force.

Feeling intimidated by growing demonstrations and unrest in the city, Charles left London, along with his wife and children. The Commons and Lords passed the Militia Bill, taking away the king's right to control his army. In June 1642 the Commons presented the Nineteen Propositions. These demands included:

● The Lords and Commons should approve all Privy Councillors.
● Laws against **Jesuits** and **recusants** should be enforced.
● The militia should be placed under parliamentary control.
● There should be sweeping reform of the church.
● Parliament should supervise the upbringing and marriage of Charles' children.

The severity of the Propositions suggested that parliament was not seriously intending to negotiate with the king. Attempts at compromise had broken down, and in July parliament voted to raise an army under the leadership of the Earl of Essex. In response, in August Charles raised his standard in Nottingham and declared war on parliament.

RAG – rate the timeline

Below are a sample exam question and a timeline. Read the question, study the timeline and, using three coloured pens, put a red, amber or green star next to the events to show:

● Red: events and policies that have no relevance to the question
● Amber: events and policies that have some significance to the question
● Green: events and policies that are directly relevant to the question.

How far do you agree that the actions of Charles I in the years 1629 to 1642 were key to the outbreak of the Civil War?

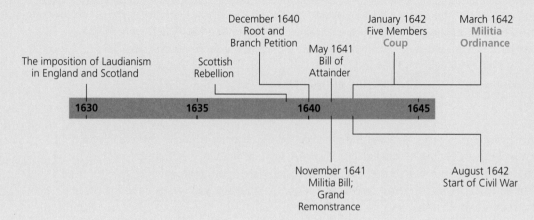

Mind map

Use the information on the opposite page to add detail to the mind map.

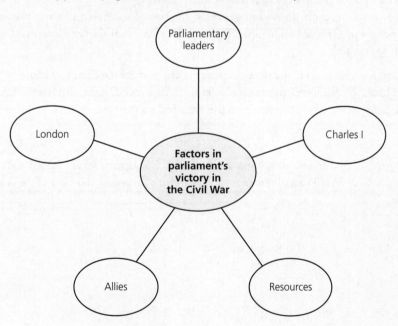

The First Civil War, 1642–46

1642

Charles was in a strong position at the outbreak of the war. He had the support of most of the nobility and the gentry, and many royalist generals were professional soldiers who had fought in the Thirty Years War (1618–48). The first major battle of the war, at Edgehill in Warwickshire, did not give either side a clear victory, but allowed royalist forces to march south, hoping to take London. The king's armies were held up at Turnham Green by a large band of volunteers who prevented the royalists from taking the capital.

1643

Royalist forces were organised to make a three-pronged attack on London from the north, the south-west and the west. However, parliament's control of the navy thwarted this plan. The naval bases of Hull, Plymouth and Gloucester provided strongholds for parliamentary forces and deterred royalist commanders from moving against London.

1644

Parliament's control of superior finances and resources began to turn the tide of war in its favour. Moreover, in 1643 the Scots had concluded the Solemn League and Covenant, promising parliament help from the Scottish army. The second major battle of the war, and the largest ever fought on English soil, took place at Marston Moor in Yorkshire and was a comprehensive victory for the parliamentary forces.

1645

Two significant developments confirmed the growing strength of the parliamentary position:
- Under the Self-Denying Ordinance, all members of parliament agreed to resign their military commands and were replaced by generals of proven military ability.
- Parliamentary forces were reorganised into a single army, the New Model Army. It was placed under the command of a professional soldier, **Sir Thomas Fairfax**, with **Oliver Cromwell** given command of the cavalry.

The New Model Army was crucial in parliament's conduct of the war. In the final key battle of the war, at Naseby in June, royalist forces were completely overwhelmed. During the rest of the year the New Model Army defeated royalist forces in the west and south-west.

1646

As royalist forces lost ground throughout the country, Charles left his stronghold at Oxford and surrendered to the Scots. Oxford fell to parliamentary forces in June, bringing the First Civil War to an end.

! Simple essay style

Below is a sample exam question. Use your own knowledge and the information on the opposite page to produce a plan for this question. Choose four general points and provide two or three pieces of specific information to support each general point.

Once you have planned your essay, write an introduction and conclusion for the essay. The introduction should list the points to be discussed in the essay. The conclusion should summarise the key points and justify which point was the most significant.

> How accurate is it to say that parliament won the First Civil War (1642–46) because it controlled greater financial resources than the royalists?

i Turning assertion into argument

Below are a sample essay question and two assertions. Read the exam question, then add a justification to each assertion to turn it into an argument.

> How significant was parliament's reorganisation of its military forces in the years 1645–46?

The Self-Denying Ordinance of 1645 had a significant impact on parliament's military capabilities because...

_____

The creation of the New Model Army in 1645 was key to parliament's success in the years 1645–46 because...

_____

The failure to reach a negotiated settlement, 1646–49 REVISED

Although Charles had surrendered to the Scots, he was not prepared to negotiate seriously with his opponents. The division between parliament's military forces, the Scots and the New Model Army, was reflected in parliament itself. The majority of MPs, the **Political Presbyterians**, had close ties with Scotland's military leaders, while the **Political Independents** were linked to MPs who were also New Model Army officers. Charles was convinced that his opponents' alliance would break down and thus strengthen his own bargaining position.

The Newcastle Propositions, 1646

In 1646 the Political Presbyterians sought a compromise with the Newcastle Propositions. These included:

- The office of bishop in the **Anglican** Church was to be abolished.
- Strict anti-Catholic laws were to be enforced.
- Parliament was to take control of the armed forces for 20 years.

Negotiations on these proposals had broken down by the end of 1646, and in January 1647 the Scots handed the king over to parliament.

The Heads of Proposals, 1647

In 1647 the Political Presbyterians considered disbanding the New Model Army without paying **arrears** of pay. This suggestion caused the army to become politicised, and it developed into a third factor in negotiations for a settlement. In June the army gained custody of the king, and presented their own proposals to him.

The Heads of Proposals was a far more moderate document than the Newcastle Propositions, which suggests that the army wanted to establish a lasting and stable settlement. Their main concern was to strengthen the power of parliament:

- Parliament should meet every two years.
- Constituencies were to be reorganised to reflect population size and local wealth.
- Anglican bishops were to remain.

While Charles was considering these proposals he was also engaged in secret discussions with the Scots. He signed an agreement with the Scots in December 1647, promising to impose Presbyterianism in England for three years in exchange for a Scottish army.

The Second Civil War, 1648

The war was short but fiercely contested by both sides. Fairfax put down royalist risings in the south of England, and in August Cromwell destroyed the Scottish army at the battle of Preston.

In the aftermath of the conflict the army leadership published the Remonstrance, declaring that the king was guilty of high treason for starting the Second Civil War, and should be put on trial. When parliament voted to continue negotiations with the king, troops arrested 45 MPs and excluded a further 186 from the Commons. This event was known as Pride's Purge.

The trial and execution of Charles I, 1649

In January 1649 Charles was tried by 135 Commissioners. He refused to accept that any court had the power to place a divinely appointed monarch on trial, and would not answer the charges made against him. The court found him guilty of all charges, and sentenced him to death. He was executed on 30 January 1649.

Support or challenge?

Below is a sample exam question which asks how far you agree with a specific statement. Below this are a series of general statements which are relevant to the question. Using your own knowledge and the information on the opposite page, decide whether these statements support or challenge the statement in the question and tick the appropriate box.

How far do you agree that the regicide was due more to the actions of Charles I in the years 1637 to 1649 than those of his opponents?

	SUPPORT	CHALLENGE
Charles' imposition of the Laudian Prayer Book in Scotland		
The Scottish Rebellion		
Charles' attempted arrest of the Five Members		
Pym and parliamentary radicalism		
Parliament's offer of the Newcastle Propositions		
Charles' refusal of the Heads of Proposals		
Pride's Purge		

Identify the concept

Below are five sample exam questions based on some of the following concepts:

- **Cause** – questions concern the reasons for something, or why something happened
- **Consequence** – questions concern the impact of an event, an action or a policy
- **Change/continuity** – questions ask you to investigate the extent to which things changed or stayed the same
- **Similarity/difference** – questions ask you to investigate the extent to which two events, actions or policies were similar
- **Significance** – questions concern the importance of an event, an action or a policy.

Read each of the questions and work out which of the concepts they are based on:

How accurate is it to say that the development of opposition to Charles I's religion since 1625 was the main reason for his eventual execution in 1649?

How accurate is it to say that the execution of Charles I was more the result of the politicisation of the New Model Army than the alienation of parliament?

To what degree was the position of Charles I stronger in 1646 than it was in 1625?

How accurate is it to say that the king's execution in 1649 was a response to the political actions rather than the religious policies of Charles I since 1637?

Republican rule, 1649–60

REVISED

In the years 1649–60 several attempts were made to
establish a stable republican regime acceptable to the
country as a whole. Each experiment failed, leading to
the Stuart restoration in 1660.

The Rump Parliament, 1649–53

After the execution of Charles I, Cromwell and his
supporters attempted to broaden support for the
government by allowing many MPs back into parliament.
This reinforced the tension between parliament and the
army due to the reintroduction of conservative MPs who
were less likely to enact reforms.

In May 1649 the Rump abolished the monarchy and
the House of Lords, and declared England to be a
Commonwealth. In the short term, the New Model
Army had to deal with the threat from Ireland and
Scotland and this delayed any confrontation with
parliament over who held power.

Ireland

Parliament feared a possible Irish invasion of England,
aimed at bringing Charles II to the throne. Cromwell
landed in Ireland in July 1649 and set about restoring
English rule. His methods were notoriously brutal.
The garrison at Drogheda was massacred because it
refused to surrender, and the town of Wexford suffered
a similar fate. Cromwell left his generals to complete the
subjugation of the country, and returned to England in
1650 to deal with the threat from Scotland.

Scotland

Scotland posed a grave threat to republican rule. Scottish
officer David Leslie commanded a powerful army which
he handed over to Charles II, provoking a third civil war.
Charles II was the son of Charles I and only had the title
Charles II by the Scots' declaration. Cromwell defeated
the Scots at Dunbar in 1650, and in 1651 he destroyed
Charles II's armies at Worcester. Following his defeat,
Charles II fled to France and spent nine years in exile.
Cromwell's successes in Ireland and Scotland ensured the
survival of the republican government, and increased the
prestige of the armed forces.

The failure of the Rump Parliament

Throughout its short life the Rump Parliament failed
to command widespread support for its rule. This was
because of:
- the conservative nature of many MPs
- limited finances – without substantial resources,
  the MPs of the Rump were less inclined to initiate
  significant reform

- the threat from Ireland and Scotland – facing a serious
  threat, the Rump had to employ its immediate
  resources and time
- fear of radical religious groups – MPs were concerned
  at the development of new groups and sought to
  reimpose religious control
- fear of the New Model Army – Pride's Purge had
  shown the MPs of the Rump that the army held
  real power
- the Dutch War – resources and time were used on war
  with the Dutch, which broke out in 1652.

In 1653 Cromwell believed that the Rump intended to
extend its life. He dissolved the Rump by force, replacing
it with the Nominated Assembly.

The Nominated Assembly, 1653

The Nominated Assembly was composed of members
nominated by the government. They were religious
radicals determined to establish **godly** rule in the
country.

The Assembly had substantial achievements to its credit:
- civil marriage was legalised
- registers for births, marriages and deaths were
  established
- the revenue system was reformed.

However, the Assembly lost the support of the political
classes with its more radical proposals, including one
to abolish the **tithe**. In December 1653 conservative
members handed back the Assembly's powers to
Cromwell.

The end of the Commonwealth, 1653

The **Instrument of Government** of 1653 was a written
constitution which aimed at giving the republic long-
term stability. The Commonwealth was replaced with
the **Protectorate**. Government was to be carried out
by a Council of State, a parliament was to be elected
every three years and Oliver Cromwell was installed
as Lord Protector.

1 The quest for political stability, 1625–88

222

Quick quizzes at **www.hoddereducation.co.uk/myrevisionnotes**

Mind map

Use the information on the opposite page to add detail to the mind map below.

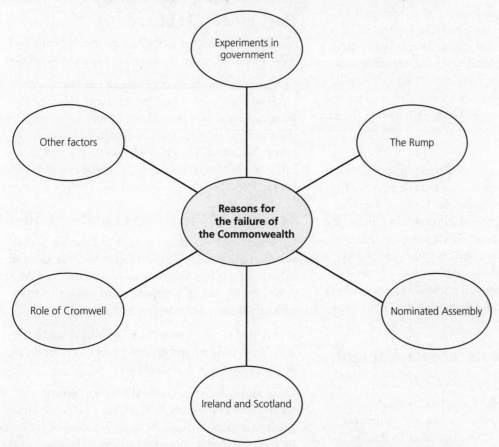

Experiments in government

Other factors

The Rump

Reasons for the failure of the Commonwealth

Role of Cromwell

Nominated Assembly

Ireland and Scotland

Simple essay style

Below is a sample exam question. Use your own knowledge and the information up to this point in the book to produce a plan for this question. Choose four general points, and provide three pieces of specific information to support each general point.

Once you have planned your essay, write the introduction and conclusion for the essay. The introduction should list the points to be discussed in the essay. The conclusion should summarise the key points and justify which point was the most important.

> How accurate is it to say that the authority of the political elite was undermined in the years 1640 to 1653?

The role of Cromwell, 1640–58

1640–49

Cromwell emerged as a national figure through his military success during the Civil War. Cromwell remained in parliament, alongside his role as an officer. It was with the New Model Army's politicisation that Cromwell became more significant. Even so, it could be argued that **Ireton**, Cromwell's son-in-law, was more of a driving force in bringing about the execution of the king.

1649–53

Following Charles' execution, Cromwell's political influence was again diverted due to the necessity of him leading campaigns against the Irish and then the Scots, for which he became commander-in-chief of the New Model Army in June 1650. It was only after the defeat of the Scots in 1651 and his return to London that Cromwell once again began to impose himself more directly on the political process. This explains the dissolution of both the Rump and the Nominated Assembly in 1653.

The First Protectorate Parliament, 1654–55

Cromwell hoped that the Protectorate would bring stability to political and national life, and secure the support of a broad spectrum of opinion. In this, he was to be bitterly disappointed.

The First Protectorate Parliament met in September 1654, and displayed none of the harmony that Cromwell had hoped for. One hundred members refused to accept the Instrument of Government (see page 30) and withdrew from parliament. Attempts were made to reduce the size of the army, and powerful attacks were mounted against the principle of religious liberty. Frustrated by the parliament's attitudes, Cromwell dissolved the assembly in January 1655.

The rule of the Major-Generals

Cromwell did not immediately call a new parliament, but instead imposed direct military rule across England. Eleven **Major-Generals** were appointed to rule different areas of the country. They were to provide military security, but Cromwell's main intention was that they would carry out a national reform of morals and behaviour. They were empowered to suppress taverns and brothels, and to punish adultery, blasphemy and drunkenness.

The Major-Generals experiment highlighted the fundamental tensions between reform and stability which characterised the entire period of republican rule.

The Second Protectorate Parliament, 1656–58

The Second Protectorate Parliament met in September 1656 and, once again, one hundred MPs were excluded.

In March 1657 parliament presented Cromwell with the **Humble Petition and Advice**, which offered the Protector the crown of England. Strong opposition from the army and religious radicals persuaded Cromwell to refuse the offer in May. He did, however, accept the office of Lord Protector for life, with the power to choose his successor.

The end of the Protectorate, 1658–60

Cromwell died in September 1658 and was succeeded by his son, Richard. The new Protector had little political experience and had no strong links with the New Model Army, the key power group. Richard was forced from office by the army's leaders in 1659.

A period of chaotic instability followed, caused by the inability of military and civilian groups to agree on the future government of the country.

Order was restored by **General George Monck**, the commander of the army in Scotland, who crossed into England in January 1660. As he marched towards London he was presented with a large number of petitions calling for the restoration of the monarchy. Elections were held for a new parliament, and the Convention Parliament met in April 1660. Parliament resolved to restore the traditional government of king, Lords and Commons, and on 29 May Charles II was welcomed on his return to London from exile abroad.

Simple essay style

Below is a sample exam question. Use your own knowledge and the information on the opposite page to produce a plan for this question. Choose four general points, and provide three pieces of specific information to support each general point.

Once you have planned your essay, write the introduction and conclusion for the essay. The introduction should list the points to be discussed in the essay. The conclusion should summarise the key points and justify which point was the most important.

> How far do you agree that military involvement in political affairs was responsible for the failure of republican government in the years 1649–60?

 Recommended reading

Below is a list of suggested further reading on this topic.
- J. Morrill, *Oliver Cromwell*, Chapter 5, Longman (2007)
- J.C. Davis. *Oliver Cromwell*, Chapter 9, Arnold (2001)
- D.L. Smith, *Oliver Cromwell*, Chapter 6, Blackwell (2010)
- B. Coward, *Oliver Cromwell*, Chapters 5–7, Longman (2000)

The Restoration Settlement, 1660–64

The Declaration of Breda, 1660

Before he returned to England, Charles II issued the Declaration of Breda. He promised:
- to listen to the advice of parliament
- an **indemnity** – people would not be persecuted for the actions they took during the civil wars, except for those who took part in the execution of Charles I or who resisted the king's return, the details of which were to be settled by parliament
- 'liberty to tender consciences' – toleration for peaceful religious beliefs, the details of which were to be settled by parliament
- settlement of disputes over land would be decided by parliament
- payment of the army's wages.

The search for stability, 1660

Charles II and the Convention Parliament attempted to ensure political stability in 1660:
- The Act of Indemnity and Oblivion granted a general pardon to supporters of the republican regimes, apart from those who had condemned Charles I to death.
- Land confiscated during the republican period was restored to its original owners.
- The Convention oversaw the peaceful disbanding of the New Model Army.
- The Anglican Church was restored, along with the bishops.

The religious settlement, 1661–64

Charles had promised religious toleration, but the ultra-royalist Cavalier Parliament, elected in 1661, was determined to restore the Anglican Church and to persecute **non-conformists**.
- 1661: The Corporation Act allowed only Anglicans to hold office in local corporations. Many corporations were Puritan strongholds, and the Act severely weakened Puritan power and influence.
- 1662: The Quaker Act imposed severe financial penalties on **Quakers**.
- 1662: The Act of Uniformity required all clergymen to accept Anglican doctrines and rituals. As a result, hundreds of parish priests were driven from their livings.
- 1664: The **Conventicle Act** forbade dissenting assemblies of more than five people.

During his reign Charles tried to change some of the harsher aspects of the religious settlement, but his actions only caused conflict between crown and parliament.

The settlement of government and finance, 1660–64

Parliament used its most influential form of power – finance – to limit Charles. On the surface, Charles received a generous settlement of £1.2 million a year and a new **Hearth Tax**, a tax on every fireplace and stove in the kingdom, was introduced in 1662. While putting Charles in a better position than early Stuart monarchs, it was not enough to make him independent. Charles was therefore always reliant on further parliamentary finance, for which he would need the consent of MPs.

In 1664 the Cavalier Parliament replaced the Triennial Act of 1641 with a much weaker version. The new Act did not establish a procedure to be followed if the king failed to call a parliament.

Spectrum of importance

Look at the following sample exam question and a list of general points which could be used to answer the question. Use your own knowledge and the information on the opposite page to reach a judgement about the importance of these general points to the question posed.

Write numbers on the spectrum below to indicate their relative importance. Having done this, write a brief justification of your placement, explaining why some of these factors are more important than others. The resulting diagram could form the basis of an essay plan.

> How successful was the Restoration Settlement of 1660–64 in establishing religious and political stability?

1 The Anglican Church

2 Laws against dissenters

3 The crown's financial settlement

4 The army

5 The Act of Indemnity and Oblivion

6 The Triennial Act, 1664.

←――――――――――――――――――――――――――――――――――――→

Least important   Most important

 Develop the detail

Below are a sample exam-style question and a paragraph written in answer to this question. The paragraph contains a limited amount of detail. Annotate the paragraph to add additional detail to the answer.

> To what extent was the Restoration Settlement of 1664 only a short-term solution to problems of government and religion?

Charles II and parliament had to deal with several major problems in 1660–64. They had to settle problems left over from the republican years. Evidence for this is the disbanding of the New Model Army. They also took steps to solve religious issues. Evidence for this is the Act of Uniformity of 1662. Parliament wanted to establish the different powers of crown and parliament. Evidence of this is the crown's financial settlement. Overall, the Restoration Settlement did not solve major problems in religion and government.

Conflicts between king and parliaments, 1665–81

REVISED

In the years 1665–81 divisions grew between king and parliament in matters of politics, religion and foreign policy.

The fall of Clarendon, 1667

Edward Hyde, 1st Earl of Clarendon, dominated political life in the early 1660s, but gave little attention to managing parliament on the king's behalf. He was held responsible for England's humiliating defeat in the Second Dutch War of 1665–67, when the Dutch attacked the English fleet in the river Medway. Charles directed parliament's anger against Clarendon, who fled to France in 1667. The removal of Clarendon as chief minister led to a group of diverse ministers fulfilling his role – **Clifford**, **Arlington**, Buckingham, Ashley and **Lauderdale** (the 'Cabal').

The Third Dutch War, 1672–74

In 1670 Charles and **Louis XIV** of France concluded the **Secret Treaty of Dover**, in which Charles agreed to join France in any future French war against the Dutch. MPs were unhappy with this agreement. They were suspicious of Charles' relationship with the absolutist and Catholic Louis, and most sympathised with the Protestant Dutch. In the secret terms of the Treaty, Charles agreed to convert to Catholicism when he felt the time was right, in return for a pension from the French.

Charles II started a Third Dutch War in 1672. Effective propaganda by the Dutch ruler, **William of Orange**, made the war very unpopular with parliament and the people. Their anger against the king only increased with the **Declaration of Indulgence** of 1672, granting a substantial measure of religious freedom to Catholics and **dissenters**. In 1672 due to the financial demands of the Dutch War Charles II had to declare himself bankrupt, known as Stop the Exchequer. After a stormy parliamentary session in 1673 Charles withdrew the Declaration. The **Test Act** of 1673 required all office holders to declare their opposition to Catholic religious doctrines. One effect of the Test Act was that the king's brother, James, Duke of York, was excluded from high office. Another was the fall of the Cabal and the subsequent emergence of Thomas Osborne, Earl of Danby, as Charles II's new chief minister.

The Exclusion Crisis, 1678–81

In 1678 a number of wild allegations were made against Catholic nobles and even the queen herself, claiming that they were planning to murder the king and place the Duke of York upon the throne. Although the 'Popish Plot' was completely fabricated, it gave parliament the opportunity to denounce the king's ministers, forcing Charles to dissolve the Cavalier Parliament in January 1679.

The Exclusion Parliaments, 1679–81

Two 'Exclusion Parliaments' met in London between 1679 and 1681, and each proposed a bill to exclude the Duke of York from the succession to the throne. The issue generated widespread political debate, supported by mass demonstrations in favour of **exclusion**. Charles refused to consider the proposed measure, and dissolved each parliament after just a few months.

A third Exclusion Parliament met in March 1681 in the royalist stronghold of Oxford. By this time Charles had received a large financial subsidy from Louis XIV, allowing him greater independence from parliament. Thus, he was able to refuse all parliament's demands, dissolving it after just a few weeks.

Whigs and Tories

The Exclusion Crisis led to the gradual emergence of two political groupings:

- The **Whigs** were those who supported exclusion. They claimed that toleration of Catholics would cause a drift towards royal absolutism, on the French model. They championed popular sovereignty and the defence of England's religion and its traditional liberties.
- The **Tories** were MPs who were strong believers in the power of the monarchy, the hereditary succession and respect for authority. They attacked the Whigs as closet republicans, whose beliefs could destabilise the country and possibly lead to a renewal of civil war.

Identify key terms

Below is a sample exam-style question which includes a key word or term. Key terms are important because their meaning can be helpful in structuring your answer, developing an argument and establishing criteria that will help form the basis of a judgement.

> How accurate is it to say that Charles II's relationship with parliament deteriorated in the years 1665 to 1681?

● First, identify the key word or term. This will be a word or phrase that is important to the meaning of the question. Underline the word or phrase.

● Second, define the key phrase. Your definition should set out the key features of the phrase or word that you are defining.

● Third, make an essay plan that reflects your definition.

● Finally, write a sentence answering the question that refers back to the definition.

Now repeat the task, and consider how the change in key terms affects the structure, argument and final judgement of your essay.

> How accurate is it to say that parliament was more powerful than Charles II in the years 1665 to 1681?

Mind map

Use the information on the opposite page to add detail to the mind map below.

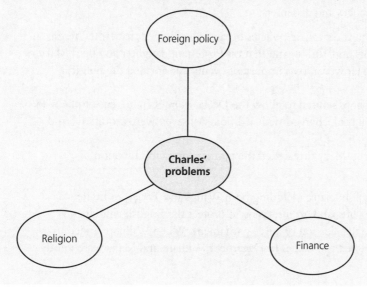

Personal Rule and the collapse of royal power, 1681–88

National agitation died down after the Oxford parliament, and Charles took a number of steps to strengthen his position:

- The Whig leader, **Shaftesbury**, fled abroad after being charged with treason.
- Local government charters were revised in order to remove Whigs from office.
- The Rye House Plot of 1683 was a conspiracy by Cromwellian officers to murder the king. The plot failed, but Charles seized the opportunity to arrest leading Whigs and further weaken his opponents.
- In 1684 Charles defied the Triennial Act by failing to summon parliament.

The collapse of the Stuart monarchy, 1685–88

Charles II died in February 1685. His brother, James, despite his open Catholicism, was in a very strong position on his accession to the throne. He had the support of the Tories and the Anglican Church, which together made up the majority of the political elite. He called parliament, which was very Tory in its outlook and which granted him substantial funding. Within three years James had dissipated their goodwill and destroyed any chances of establishing political stability under the Stuart monarchy. In 1688, for the second time in 40 years, a Stuart king would be forcibly removed from the throne.

During his short reign, James displayed an extraordinary lack of political judgement in supporting Catholicism openly.

- He appointed Catholics to a number of offices, including the Privy Council and university fellowships, and as officers in the army.
- Over 200 Catholics replaced Protestants as Justices of the Peace (JPs).
- James tried to broaden his support in 1687 with the Declaration of Indulgence, which suspended laws against both Catholics and dissenters.

The political classes were prepared to accept these policies because they hoped that James' reign would not last long (James was in his mid-fifties), and that his Protestant daughter and heir, Mary, would reverse his Catholic policies. However, two important events transformed the political scene:

- In April 1688 seven Anglican bishops refused to allow the Declaration of Indulgence to be read in their churches and were put on trial, charged with sedition. All seven were acquitted amid widespread public celebrations.
- In June the birth of a son to Queen Mary threatened the permanent establishment of Catholicism in England.

These two events led seven leading politicians, including both Whigs and Tories, to invite William of Orange, Princess Mary's husband, to intervene to protect the English church and the country's liberties and to ensure the election of a free parliament. When William landed in November, James lost his nerve and fled to France. In December William and Mary were jointly offered the crown.

Complete the paragraph

Below are a sample exam-style question and a paragraph written in answer to this question. The paragraph contains a point and a concluding explanatory link back to the question, but lacks detail. Complete the paragraph, adding detail in the space provided.

To what extent did fear of Catholicism in the years from 1678 lead to the fall of James II in 1688?

From 1678 there was increasing tension over the heir to the throne, James, Duke of York, being a Catholic. Yet the situation in England in 1685 when James came to the throne was remarkably calm given the previous tension over exclusion in the years 1678 to 1681. James succeeded, however, in alienating the political elite. . .

_____

_____

 Recommended reading

Below is a list of suggested further reading on the Glorious Revolution.

- T. Harris, *Revolution: The Great Crisis of the British Monarchy, 1685–1720*, Chapter 8, Penguin (2007)
- D. Scott, *Leviathan. The Rise of Britain as a Great Power*, pages 234–253, Collins (2014)
- J. Miller, *The Glorious Revolution*, pages 17–55, Routledge (1997)
- S.C. Pincus, *England's Glorious Revolution: A Brief History with Documents*, Bedford/St. Martin's (2006)

Exam focus

Below is are a sample exam-style essay question and a model answer. Read it and the comments around it.

How successful was Charles II in dealing with the problems he faced in the years 1667 to 1678?

In the eleven years from 1667 to 1678 Charles II faced a range of problems. These included finance, religion, foreign policy and, to a degree, the ministers of the Cabal. All impacted on Charles' relationship with parliament and were interrelated. His financial weakness stemmed from his foreign policy, and parliament was able to exploit this to shape his religious policy. While Charles dealt with these problems in a pragmatic way, it was his lack of financial strength that created the greatest problems for him, as was clearly illustrated by the 1672 Stop of the Exchequer. Charles' political skill, however, saw him manage these problems and emerge by 1678 in a stronger position than in 1667.

> This is a direct, brief and clear introduction which addresses the specific question and is strengthened by reference to the specific example of the 1672 declaration of bankruptcy.

The very nature of Charles' government in the years 1667 to 1673 could be seen as a problem for him. The removal of Clarendon as chief minister led to a group of diverse ministers fulfilling his role: Clifford, Arlington, Buckingham, Ashley and Lauderdale (the Cabal). This meant there was no clear direction to policy from Charles' ministers. However, the diverse nature of the Cabal was, to a degree, an advantage to Charles, as it enabled him to appear as a symbol of unity. It could be argued that while the nature of the Cabal created a lack of direction, Charles was more successful in maintaining his authority over these diverse ministers than over Clarendon.

> This is a clear paragraph that explains the problem of lack of direction caused by the nature of the Cabal but balances this with how it worked, personally, to reinforce Charles' authority.

Charles II encountered financial and foreign policy problems during his reign. To fund the Dutch war Charles needed money from parliament. In 1672 the king declared himself bankrupt and 'stopped the Exchequer'. In 1674 he made peace with the Dutch. In 1670, in order to try and secure more funds, Charles signed the Secret Treaty of Dover. In return for receiving a pension from the French, Charles agreed to convert to Catholicism (when he felt ready) and support the French in their war with the Dutch. France was fairly successful against the Dutch, and in light of this, £600,000 for the navy was approved by parliament in 1677. Any further money was conditional on an alliance against France. Charles believed parliament was threatening his prerogative. By 1678 it could be argued that Charles had improved his financial position by declaring peace with the Dutch and also by taking advantage of his personal links with his cousin, Louis XIV. In turn, the Treaty of Dover also gave him an advantage in his relationship with parliament. By 1678 he knew he was less dependent on parliament for funds and therefore had successfully put himself in a more secure position.

> This paragraph matches the wording of the question and uses appropriate evidence.

Religion was another problem for Charles in this period. Like foreign policy, it was related to the issue of finance and thereby his relationship with parliament. Charles wanted the Declaration of Indulgence passed and to allow Catholics more freedom. However, Presbyterian Anglicans wanted a narrow church based on Anglican views. Using financial persuasion, parliament was able to force Charles to sign the Test Act in 1673, which prevented Catholics from gaining political power. In 1673, as a result of the Test Act, the Cabal collapsed. Another consequence of the Test Act was that the heir to the throne's Catholic religion became publicly known. James, Duke of York's Catholicism greatly worried parliament and from 1673 onwards MPs tried to exclude James from succession. By using their influence over finance, parliament were a real problem for Charles as they were able to shape religious policy. Charles failed in his religious policy and the issue of James' Catholicism became an even greater source of tension between crown and parliament after 1678, in the so-called Exclusion Crisis.

> This paragraph demonstrates a clear judgement about Charles' failure with regard to his aims in religion. Relevant reference beyond the period to add to the judgement is also valid.

In the years 1673 to 1678 Charles' government continued to impact negatively on his relationship with parliament. After the collapse of the Cabal, Danby became Charles' chief minister, and improved the financial position of Charles through his restraint as

Lord Treasurer. Danby also improved Charles' relationship with parliament by essentially creating a loyal support group in parliament using crown patronage. However, by 1678 Danby had become a problem for Charles. His role as 'Bribe-Master General' worried some MPs as it appeared to show the growing potential for the crown to manipulate the influence of parliament. MPs also worried that Charles was becoming too independent and would turn absolutist like his French cousin, King Louis XIV. Despite Danby's financial success, he couldn't control Charles' spending and between 1674 and 1679 debt increased by £750,000. Thus by 1678 Charles still had a problem with the direction of his government.

> The opening sentence is directly focused on the wording of the question. There could be more developed comment on the evidence/narrative in the paragraph in order to achieve a higher level.

Direct opposition was a limited problem for Charles in the years 1667 to 1678. Republicanism was discredited and Charles' persecution limited most potential threats. The biggest threat to Charles actually came from a group known as the 'country', who should have been Charles' key support. The 'country' was essentially the gentry and had real power, as in reality they controlled most of the land and ran the country on a practical day-to-day basis. The political class was also conservative and favoured parliament over absolutism. Thus the most problematic opposition to Charles came from the Political Nation through parliament. When Charles ruled in line with their values he was more secure, but when he deviated – for example, in trying to broaden the church – they could use the financial influence of parliament to successfully oppose him, as with the 1673 Test Act.

> The recognition of the influence of the Political Nation illustrates the candidate's appreciation of where real power lay in early modern England and the real source of problems for Charles II.

Charles II faced a wide range of problems in the eleven years from the fall of Clarendon in 1667 to the start of the Exclusion Crisis in 1678. These issues – finance, religion, financial policy and the threat of opposition – were not new. Indeed, they had beset many monarchs before Charles. While Charles was under the influence of parliament and Louis XIV because of his financial problems, he can be seen as a success in that he managed these problems and maintained a religious settlement with the agreement of the Political Nation. From Charles' own perspective he was a success, as his main aim was to remain on the throne. While he still faced a range of problems in 1678 there had been no serious threat to his power. However, Charles' pragmatic response to these problems proved successful only in the short term. From a long-term perspective, Charles arguably failed to deal with problems relating to the Stuarts, and more structural problems were only dealt with when William III came to the throne in 1688.

> This conclusion shows a clear conceptual understanding and wider knowledge of the period.

Some key issues relevant to the question are addressed and there is a range of evidence deployed to show understanding of the demands of the question. More sustained analysis and a more fully developed illustration of the themes and concepts of the question would strengthen the response.

Providing explanation

It is useful to look at this answer through the eyes of the examiner. The examiner will look for a range of explanations. In the margin, write a word or phrase which sums up each specific explanation as it appears. Good answers present at least three explanations and discuss each one in a separate paragraph. Also, highlight or underline where any attempts are made to show links between explanations or where prioritisation occurs.

AS-level questions

Were Charles I's actions the main reason for political instability in the years 1625 to 1642?

To what extent were the problems of government faced by Charles II in the years 1660 to 1685 caused most by the limits of his finance?

Laud's policies and religious uniformity

The Anglican Church had been established by Elizabeth I as a 'middle way' between Catholicism and European Protestantism. Many traditional features of Catholic worship had been retained, such as priests' vestments and incense, but Anglican beliefs reflected the teachings of the Swiss reformer John Calvin. The 'middle way' was an uneasy compromise, but it ensured religious peace for many years.

By 1625 there were growing divisions within Anglicanism about the church's beliefs and practices:

- Arminianism was a set of beliefs which promoted church services involving rituals and formal ceremony. Arminians followed the traditional Catholic belief in free will, which meant that individuals could choose whether or not to follow a path to salvation (see page 6).
- Puritans were Anglicans who opposed rituals and priestly vestments. They wanted to purify services by promoting simplicity rather than ceremony. Puritans were also concerned for people's moral improvement and supported action against moral misbehaviour, such as adultery and drunkenness. They also believed in the **Calvinist** doctrine of predestination – that God had already chosen those who would be saved, regardless of their behaviour during their lifetime (see page 8).

William Laud, a prominent Arminian, was appointed Archbishop of Canterbury in 1633. He worked to impose greater religious uniformity on church services:

- The communion table was moved to the east end of the church, and was railed off from the congregation.
- Vestments and incense were to be used in services, and hymns and sacred music were encouraged.
- Stained-glass windows were to be installed in churches.

These Arminian measures angered the Puritans because they stressed the outward forms of worship. Puritans believed that Laud was moving the church in the direction of Catholicism. Laud further offended the Puritans by issuing the Book of Sports in 1633, which allowed people to participate in traditional sports and pastimes on Sundays.

Many people welcomed Laud's reforms because they imposed fewer demands on those who attended Sunday services. They also approved of the reduction in the number of sermons, which were popular with the Puritans.

The imposition of Laudianism

To ensure that Laud's measures were imposed, visitations by the agents of bishops in their **dioceses** were conducted more thoroughly and there is evidence of the records of these visitations being personally reviewed by Laud and Charles. Laud made use of the church courts, notably the **Court of High Commission** to punish, through fines or imprisonment, those who refused to implement Laudianism.

Many Puritan clergy were unable to accept the changes to church services. After 1633 thousands of clergy, along with many of their followers, emigrated to the American colonies, where they could worship freely without fear of persecution.

Many of the gentry also opposed Laud's actions. These men were often strongly Calvinist, and regarded Laud's innovations as disrupting the Elizabethan 'middle way'. Their opposition grew with the trial of Prynne, Bastwick and Burton in 1637. They were middle-class professionals charged with smuggling anti-Arminian tracts from abroad and publishing attacks on the bishops. They were sentenced to have their ears mutilated and were imprisoned for life. Laud's opponents believed that the harsh sentences were out of proportion to their offences. Attacks on Laud were to figure prominently in the meeting of the Long Parliament in 1640.

Simple essay style

Below is a sample exam question. Use your own knowledge and the information on the opposite page to produce a plan for this question. Choose four general points, and provide three pieces of specific information to support each general point. Once you have planned your essay, write the introduction and conclusion for the essay. The introduction should list the points to be discussed in the essay. The conclusion should summarise the key points and justify which point was the most important.

> How accurate is it to say Laud's Arminian policies weakened the Church of England in the period 1633–40?

Developing an argument a

Below are a sample A-level exam-style question, a list of key points to be made in the essay and a paragraph from the essay. Read the question, the plan and the sample paragraph. Rewrite the paragraph in order to develop an argument. Your paragraph should explain why the factor discussed in the paragraph is linked to the question.

> How successful were Laud's attempts to impose religious uniformity on the Church of England in the years 1633–40?

Key points:

- Laud's Arminian measures
- The imposition of Laud's measures
- Support for Laud's reforms
- Calvinist opposition
- The extent of opposition by 1640

Sample paragraph:

During the 1630s Archbishop Laud introduced a series of reforms within the Anglican Church. He did not reform the church's doctrines, but wanted uniformity in religious services. Laud's measures provoked little opposition from most people, but many Puritans were not prepared to accept them, and a large number of Puritans actually emigrated to America in order to worship in their own way. However, the opposition of the largely Calvinist gentry limited the success of Laud's actions, and their grievances featured prominently when the Long Parliament met in 1640.

The Church of England, 1640–62

In the years to 1640 the Church of England played a key role in the political and social life of the country. The years 1640–60 saw the virtual destruction of the Church of England as the centre of religious life.

Parliament's reordering of the church, 1640–53

From 1643 parliament introduced a series of measures to reform the Church of England:
- The office of bishop was abolished in favour of a **Presbyterian** form of government, which meant that church rule was carried out by organisations of deacons and local elders.
- The Book of Common Prayer was banned and was replaced by the Directory of Worship.
- Arminian features of churches, such as stained glass and statues, were removed.
- Traditional Christian festivals such as Christmas and Easter were no longer celebrated. Instead, they became days of fasting and prayer.
- In 1650 a Toleration Act ended the requirement of compulsory attendance at the national church's services.

These changes led to thousands of parish priests being expelled from their homes. Many bishops were imprisoned or exiled, or simply went into hiding.

The Cromwellian Church, 1653–60

One of Cromwell's key aims was to bring about a religious and social reformation, which meant establishing godly rule and an improvement in public morality on the lines suggested by the Puritans.

The Instrument of Government of 1653 was England's first written constitution. As well as establishing the republican form of government, it granted liberty of worship to all except Catholics and the more extreme Protestant sects.

The restoration of Anglicanism, 1660–62

The Restoration in May 1660 restored the Anglican Church, as well as the Stuart monarchy. Charles II had demonstrated in the Declaration of Breda that he favoured religious toleration for non-conformists and Catholics. The king and his chief minister, Clarendon, sought to broaden the Church of England to accommodate moderate Protestant groups that had emerged during and after the Civil War. In 1661 the Savoy House Conference met to discuss the issue, but members of the Cavalier Parliament opposed the toleration offered at Breda. Instead they imposed a narrow religious settlement that became known as the Clarendon Code:
- The Corporation Act of 1661 required all involved in local government to be communicant members of the Church of England.
- The Act of Uniformity of 1662 made the Book of Common Prayer compulsory in all churches.
- Under the Conventicle Act of 1664, religious meetings of five or more people were forbidden.
- The Five Mile Act of 1665 established that clergymen who had been expelled from their parish for refusing to conform to the Act of Uniformity could not go within five miles of their former parish.

Neither Clarendon nor the king supported the narrow and vindictive religious settlement, but they were forced to agree to parliament's wishes. Two thousand clergy were deprived of their livings for refusing the Act of Uniformity – many of these followed the example of previous Puritans and emigrated to America.

Although the Anglican Church had been restored in the 1660s, it could no longer pretend to have exclusive control over the country's religious beliefs. Despite the persecution of religious dissenters, non-conformists remained a significant minority within many parts of the country.

Complete the paragraph

Below are a sample exam question and a paragraph written in answer to this question. The paragraph contains a point and specific examples, but lacks a concluding analytical link back to the question. Complete the paragraph, adding this link in the space provided.

To what extent were religious tensions in England reduced in the years 1640–60?

Challenges to the authority of Charles I and the Church of England from 1640 allowed free expression of religious ideas that had previously been suppressed. The civil war and revolution merely brought further development of radical ideas and the emergence of new religious groups. Parliament in the years from 1640 sought to broaden the church and allow more freedom for such groups to worship freely.

_____

_____

Turning assertion into argument

Below are a sample exam question and a series of assertions. Read the exam question and then add a justification to each of the assertions to turn it into an argument.

How accurate is it to say that the Restoration's religious settlement created more problems than it solved?

Charles' aim of religious toleration was unrealistic.

_____

_____

The Restoration's religious settlement was shaped by parliament, not by Charles.

_____

_____

The Restoration's religious settlement brought stability.

_____

_____

The growth of religious non-conformity: Puritanism under Charles I

Puritans were members of the Church of England who opposed Elizabeth I's 'middle way'. They remained within the church because they supported Anglican doctrines which reflected the views of John Calvin. However, they were strong opponents of the rituals of Anglican services, which they believed retained too many features of Catholic worship. They wanted further reforms that would implement a more purified and Protestant form of worship.

Puritan opposition

Puritans opposed most of Laud's policies which promoted the Arminian beliefs on the 'beauty of holiness'. They suspected that Laud and Charles were both determined to restore Catholicism as England's official religion.

Puritan opposition, though strong in London and in provinces such as East Anglia, was not often expressed openly. Many Puritans were politically conservative, and the gentry knew that they had much to lose from opposing the king. The imposition of Arminianism also limited the scope for Puritan opposition:

- Puritan books and pamphlets were censored, and texts brought from abroad were seized and destroyed.
- Although predestination was a part of Anglican doctrine, preaching on predestination was banned.
- Puritan preachers were no longer financed by town councils or by individuals.

It was only the most committed Puritans who were prepared to openly oppose Laudianism:

- In 1633 the Puritans of the parish of St Gregory's in London unsuccessfully tried to use the courts to oppose Charles' policy of railing off the altar.
- In 1638 the Puritan **John Lilburne** was whipped through the streets of London for distributing anti-Laudian pamphlets.

Open opposition to Laudianism from the Puritans was rare. Many reluctantly accepted the reforms of the 1630s and waited for better times. Others simply chose to emigrate.

Emigration

It is estimated that 80,000 Puritans emigrated from England during the 1630s. Many settled in Ireland, the West Indies and the Dutch Republic, and around 20,000 settled in the American colony of Massachusetts. Whole families migrated together in search of the religious freedom that Laud's policies denied them.

With the breakdown of Charles' authority after the religion-inspired rebellion of Presbyterian Scots in 1637, some Puritans began to return from overseas. When Charles recalled parliament in 1640, opposition to him among MPs was led by Puritans such as John Pym.

Eliminate irrelevance

Below are a sample exam question and a paragraph written in answer to this question. Read the paragraph and identify parts of the paragraph that are not directly relevant to the question. Draw a line through the information that is irrelevant and justify your deletions in the margin.

> How accurate is it to say that Puritans were a serious threat to the authority of Charles I in the years 1628 to 1638?

When Charles I came to throne in 1625 he was determined to move the Church of England towards Arminianism. With the appointment of William Laud as Bishop of London in 1628, Charles' imposition of Arminianism gathered pace. Puritans already saw the measures taken by Charles as a drift towards Catholicism, and the more aggressive implementation of Laudianism in the 1630s further increased their fears about Charles' intentions. In the 1630s some Puritans led opposition to Charles' altar policy. Other radical Puritans distributed pamphlets attacking Charles' Laudian policies. Many Puritans, however, chose to emigrate to the Dutch Republic or New England. In doing so they were showing that they were opposed to Charles' Laudianism, but they were also accepting that there was little they could do about it.

 Simple essay style   **a**

Below is a sample exam question. Use your own knowledge and the information on the opposite page to produce a plan for this question. Choose four general points, and provide three pieces of specific information to support each general point.

Once you have planned your essay, write the introduction and conclusion for the essay. The introduction should list the points to be discussed in the essay. The conclusion should summarise the key points and justify which point was the most important.

> How accurate is it to say that Puritanism was not a serious threat to Charles I in the years 1625 to 1638?

Presbyterians and religious radicalism

Charles' policies towards Scotland

In 1625 Charles I became king of England and also king of Scotland, but he did not visit Scotland for his coronation until 1633. His elaborate coronation was not designed to win the support of the Scottish elite, who were predominantly Presbyterian and strongly opposed to Arminianism. During his visit to Scotland in 1633, Charles announced his intention to replace the Scottish Prayer Book so that there would be uniformity of religious practice in both England and Scotland. Scottish Presbyterians regarded this as a threat to their independence, and they prepared to resist Charles' policy.

The Scottish Rebellion

On 23 July 1637 the Laudian Prayer Book was read for the first time in Scotland. It triggered widespread opposition across Scotland, known as the Scottish Rebellion. The aim of the Presbyterian Scots was to show Charles that he should withdraw it and cease his meddling in what they regarded as their area of influence. In 1638, 300,000 Scots signed the National Covenant in protest against Charles' actions. Charles was determined to crush the growing National Covenant movement that arose out of the Scottish Rebellion, but this merely escalated the revolt to become the Bishops' Wars, which some regard as the start of the British civil wars.

Religious radicalism

The Scottish Rebellion weakened Charles' authority over church and state and was a key factor leading to the outbreak of civil war in 1642. During and after the civil war, religious divisions multiplied, with the creation of a number of radical religious groups.

Radical religious groups

Baptists believed in adult, rather than infant, baptism. They separated from the Church of England and preached that only those 'born again' through adult baptism would attain salvation.

Ranters included a number of radical writers. They were not an organised group but they rejected all forms of organised religion, and even rejected the concept of sin.

Millenarians believed that Jesus would soon return to earth and reign for 1,000 years.

Muggletonians were followers of Lodowicke Muggleton and John Reeve who, after the execution of Charles I, claimed that the end of the world was imminent.

Fifth Monarchists were radical millenarians who, by 1650, had formed into a political grouping under **Major-General Thomas Harrison**.

Quakerism

Quakerism was the most significant form of religious radicalism that developed in the 1650s. Quakerism was significant for two reasons:
- By the late 1650s the Quaker movement had grown to about 50,000 members.
- Before 1660 the Quaker movement was willing to take direct political action. The commitment to political action included a willingness to use violence if necessary to achieve their aims.

The development of Quakerism was linked to the New Model Army in that many Quakers had served in the army. Fear of the Quakers increased after 1658. As political order broke down following Cromwell's death, Quaker numbers increased and their chief patron, the New Model Army **General Lambert**, became more influential. Restoration of the monarchy was seen by the political elite as a way of reimposing order and removing the threat of a military dictatorship under Lambert, based on Quaker support.

Quick quizzes at **www.hoddereducation.co.uk/myrevisionnotes**

! Mind map

Use the information on the opposite page to add detail to the mind map below to help your understanding of how religious radicalism developed.

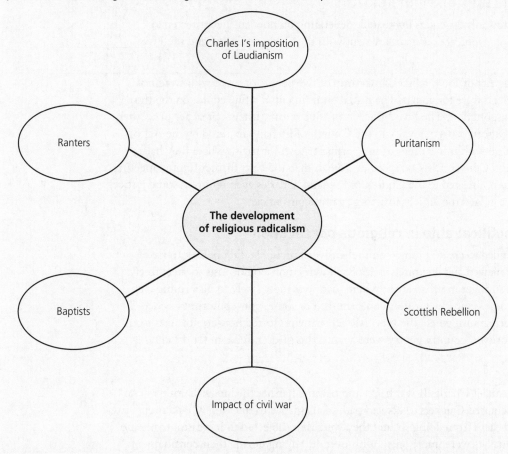

i Develop the detail **a**

Below are a sample exam-style question and a paragraph written in answer to this question. The paragraph contains a limited amount of detail. Annotate the paragraph to add additional detail to the answer.

How accurate is it to say that the Prayer Book Rebellion was a serious threat to Charles' authority in both Scotland and England?

In 1625 Charles I became king of England and king of Scotland but he did not visit Scotland for a formal coronation until 1633. This indicated to the Scots where his priorities were. Charles further compounded this during 1633 by making public his intention to remodel religion in Scotland.

The persecution of dissenters under Charles II and James II

Charles II: the religious persecutor

Charles II's approach towards dissenters fluctuated, depending on how far they threatened religious order. He took strong action against dissent with the Conventicle Act and the Five Mile Act.

Under the Conventicle Act of 1664, religious meetings of five people or more who were not in the Church of England were forbidden. The initial punishment of a fine could, on the third occasion, result in transportation. The Five Mile Act of 1665 meant that any preacher or teacher who refused the compulsory oaths of loyalty to the Church of England required by the Act of Uniformity could not go within five miles of any corporate town or parish where they had taught. In 1670 a second Conventicle Act, more draconian than the first, further limited meetings of religious gatherings not related to the Church of England. Charles even removed some Justices of the Peace who were judged too lenient in acting against conventicles.

The role of the political elite in religious persecution

Charles II always intended to create a more comprehensive church. He did not seek to have the Conventicle Act renewed and it expired in 1668, allowing non-conformists to meet freely. Generally dissent was stronger in urban areas, where there was more likely to be a ruling elite with shared ideas or some sympathy for non-conformists. For some, non-conformity was a link to the recent Interregnum, where the New Model Army protected non-conformists from persecution. The majority of country gentry were against this greater freedom for dissenters.

Quakers

Persecution of dissent under Charles II was harsh and became harsher the longer he ruled. The Quaker Act of 1662 required Quakers to take an oath of allegiance to the king. Quaker religious convictions prevented them from doing so, and they were thus subjected to increasingly intense persecution. Many Quakers were imprisoned, with over 400 dying during their confinement.

James II

James II was a strong supporter of religious toleration. He had promoted religious freedom in the American colonies and he helped his friend, the prominent Quaker William Penn, to establish the Quaker colony of Pennsylvania.

James promoted toleration with the Declaration of Indulgence of 1687, which freed Catholics and Protestant non-conformists from their religious restrictions. Many Anglicans saw the declaration as a threat to the position of the Church of England, and did not carry out its terms. A second Declaration was issued in 1688, and James ordered it to be read in all churches. However, many dissenters did not trust James, believing that his real intention was to favour Catholics. The Declarations of Indulgence were to be one of the causes of the **Glorious Revolution**, the removal of the Catholic James II and his replacement by the Protestants William and Mary.

Identify key terms

Below is a sample exam-style question which includes a key word or term. Key terms are important because their meaning can be helpful in structuring your answer, developing an argument and establishing criteria that will help form the basis of a judgement.

> How significant a threat were religious dissenters to the authority of Charles II and James II in the years 1660–88?

- First, identify the key word or term. This will be a word or phrase that is important to the meaning of the question. Underline the word or phrase.
- Second, define the key word or term. Your definition should set out the key features of the phrase or word that you are defining.
- Third, make an essay plan that reflects your definition.
- Finally, write a sentence answering the question that refers back to the definition.

Now repeat the task, and consider how the change in key terms affects the structure, argument and final judgement of your essay.

> How successful were Charles II and James II in dealing with religious dissenters in the years 1660–88?

Support your judgement

Below are a sample exam question and two basic judgements. Read the exam question and the two judgements. Support the judgement that you agree with most strongly by adding a reason that justifies the judgement.

> How accurate is it to say that by 1688 both Charles II and James II had strengthened their authority over religion?

Overall, Charles II and James II had strengthened their authority over religion by agreeing with the decisions made by parliament to maintain a relatively narrow Church of England.

_____

_____

Generally, Charles II was able to create a church that parliament supported, but James steadily undermined his relationship with the political classes by seeking to extend freedom to Catholics and dissenters.

_____

_____

Tip: Whichever option you choose, you will have to weigh up both sides of the argument. You could use phrases such as 'whereas' or words like 'although' in order to help the process of evaluation.

The Catholic question, 1625–88

Anti-Catholicism was a key theme through the seventeenth century. Catholics made up between 2 per cent and 5 per cent of the population, and in Stuart England they were subject to several penal laws. They could be fined heavily for failing to attend Anglican services, and were banned from holding military or political offices. These laws were not enforced very rigorously, however, and most Catholics lived harmoniously with their neighbours. Most people were not opposed to Catholic religious doctrines, but anti-Catholic feeling could flare up suddenly, depending on the current political situation. During the course of the seventeenth century Catholicism became increasingly associated with political absolutism, leading to suspicions that the Stuart kings intended to abolish parliamentary government and establish absolutist rule, on the French model.

Catholic influence within Charles I's court

Anti-Catholic feeling increased in the 1630s. Laud's reforms were regarded as taking the Church of England in the direction of Catholicism, and politicians were concerned at the role of Catholicism within Charles I's court.

- Queen Henrietta Maria was an ardent Catholic, and openly attended mass at court. She exerted a strong influence on Charles and on many courtiers. Daily masses were held at Somerset House, which attracted large crowds of people.
- Catholicism became popular at court, with many members of the Privy Council identified as Catholics.
- The popular impression that the government was adopting a pro-Catholic line led to a widespread rumour that the Pope had offered to make Archbishop Laud a cardinal.
- Papal envoys visited Charles from 1634, and in 1637 George Con arrived in London as an official papal ambassador.

The increase in Catholic influence at court coincided with the period of Personal Rule, which further linked Catholicism with absolutism among many of the population.

The exclusion of Catholics from religious toleration

There was little active hostility towards Catholics during the republican period. Although anti-Catholic laws were not repealed, Cromwell did not carry out any persecution of Catholics. However, he used the general fear of Catholics to promote republican virtues. During the 1650s the Duke of Savoy used Catholic troops to carry out massacres of Protestants within his state. Cromwell made sure that these acts of butchery were widely reported in newspapers and pamphlets.

Anti-Catholic sentiment, 1660–88

Anti-Catholic feeling became a constant theme during the reigns of Charles II and James II. Charles' Catholic wife, Catherine of Braganza, came to England with 30 Catholic priests, and helped to re-establish Catholic influence within the court.

From the 1660s onwards the power of France and its absolutist ruler Louis XIV gradually increased, as Louis' many wars made France one of the leading states in Europe. Charles formed an alliance with Louis against the Protestant Dutch in 1670, which led to the Third Dutch War of 1672–74. Many MPs used the opportunity afforded by the war to attack Catholic influences at court. The Test Act of 1673, which excluded Catholics from military and civil offices, forced the Duke of York to resign his military command.

Anti-Catholic feelings reached their height with the Popish Plot of 1678. Titus Oates, a former Jesuit, claimed to have uncovered a plot organised by the Jesuits to murder Charles, place his brother James on the throne and restore Catholicism in England. Over time Oates' accusations became more sensational, even implicating the queen and the Catholic Archbishop of Armagh. In 1681 opinion turned against Oates and he was imprisoned for sedition. Although the plot was a complete fabrication, the fact that it was widely believed showed how anti-Catholic feeling had spread to all classes of society.

Support or challenge?

Below is a sample exam question which asks how far you agree with a specific statement. Below this are a series of general statements which are relevant to the question. Using your own knowledge and the information on the opposite page, decide whether these statements support or challenge the statement in the question and tick the appropriate box.

	SUPPORT	CHALLENGE
Charles I's imposition of Laudianism		
Prominent individuals at court		
Charles II's links with Louis XIV		
Fear of James II		

 Simple essay style   **a**

Below is a sample exam question. Use your own knowledge and the information on the opposite page to produce a plan for this question. Choose four general points, and provide three pieces of specific information to support each general point.

Once you have planned your essay, write the introduction and conclusion for the essay. The introduction should list the points to be discussed in the essay. The conclusion should summarise the key points and justify which point was the most important.

> To what extent was the Glorious Revolution merely the high point of anti-Catholicism in the years 1660 to 1688?

Exam focus

Below are a sample exam-style essay question and a model answer. Read it and the comments around it.

How far was anti-Catholicism a source of instability for the later Stuart monarchs in the years 1660 to 1688?

Anti-Catholicism was a source of instability for the later Stuart monarchs, as it was the factor that placed most political pressure upon them. In the early years of his reign, Charles II's court was viewed negatively because of its Catholic style and there was concern about his links with his French Catholic cousin, Louis XIV. After it became clear that James, heir to the throne, was a Catholic, anti-Catholicism became even more prominent as a source of instability, building up to the Exclusion Crisis and then driving the Glorious Revolution.

> This is a good introduction that tries to address the specific question directly by using the wording of the question.

During the restoration the Political Nation remained fearful of Catholicism, and this only worsened in this period, as France became the most powerful European monarchy. Already concerned by Charles II's links with his absolutist Catholic cousin Louis XIV, the prominent Catholics at the king's court and its Catholic baroque style, parliament imposed a narrow church settlement that protected their interests. This created political instability in the political elite's relationship with Charles by making clear their concern at his apparent pro-Catholic approach.

> There is much that is good in this paragraph. It shows, for example, good conceptual understanding. It references some good detail but does so more to support comment than narrative. There is some direct shaping to the question.

In the years 1660–88 parliament was clearly anti-Catholic, and this created political instability in their working relationship with the crown. Charles' Act of Indulgence showed his Catholic affiliation, along with his declaration of war on the Protestant Dutch. In response, parliament's use of finance as their chief source of influence allowed the passage of the Test Act (1673). This Act was yet another illustration of the lack of freedoms Catholics had.

> This paragraph would benefit from commenting more directly on the question.

The Exclusion Crisis of 1678–83 was one of the high points of early modern anti-Catholicism and created instability for the Stuart monarchy. The attempted plot by radicals to exclude the future Catholic monarch, James, Duke of York from the throne, the Popish Plot (1678) and the use of pamphlets, petitions and prosecutions by the Whigs represented the apex of popular anti-Catholicism after the Restoration. However, the Glorious Revolution can also be seen as the endpoint of the Exclusion Crisis, as it reduced doubts about the religious leanings of Charles II and James II.

> This paragraph shows an appreciation of the importance of the Exclusion Crisis as a key example of anti-Catholicism, but more could be made of the real political instability it caused in the years 1678 to 1683.

The popular involvement in the calls for exclusion created real instability, as the Political Nation feared a repeat of the events of 1641 – that is, popular radicalism leading to civil war and revolution. The use of petitions, pamphlets and processions as methods of propaganda by the Whigs in the exclusion movement was arguably the largest surge of anti-Catholic propaganda in the seventeenth century. Petitions calling for the defence of Protestantism, along with pamphlets and processions attacking James and the Pope, put pressure on the crown. The Whigs stirred up popular anti-Catholic feeling as a deliberate part of their attempts to exclude James from the throne.

> As with the previous paragraph, more could be done to shape this paragraph to illustrate the instability provoked by the Exclusion Crisis.

The Popish Plot accelerated the Exclusion Crisis and the fear of Catholicism. Thus the new parliament, which met on 6 March 1679, was a very different body from the pre-1678 parliament. The tense atmosphere was a source of political instability. The first 'Exclusion Parliament' attempted to use finance as a chief source of influence to try to secure freedom rights in the event of a Catholic succession. It offered £200,000 to disband the army. An Exclusion Bill was presented by parliament in May, but ultimately the movement failed, as the necessity of removing a Catholic monarch was questioned – not because of a reversal of anti-Catholicism, but more a realisation that the damage a short-lived Catholic monarch could do was limited. All of this created political instability as the elite became split between the developing groups of Whigs (supporters of exclusion) and Tories (supporters of the succession). The political instability provoked by exclusion led to the development of a more recognisable party political system.

The Glorious Revolution was the climax of early modern anti-Catholicism in England. The political instability had reached such a point that the Political Nation was willing to accept a foreign invasion to restore order. In an effort to achieve complete toleration of Catholicism, James shifted away from Tory-Anglicans, and in 1686 introduced his Declaration of Indulgence (April 1687), suspending parliament's Test Act and softening penal laws. However, his attempt to secure a loyal parliament through a polling process provoked real political instability. James' Declaration created a reaction, seen in Louis XIV's Revocation of the Edict of Nantes and William of Orange and Mary's statement of support for the Test Act. Support for the Test Act increased as conspiracy theorists witnessed the influx of Huguenots and linked France and England as two absolute powers. As a result, the Political Nation became more alienated from James II.

The political instability created by James II's policies between 1685 and 1688 forced the political elite to lead a revolution, backed by foreign invasion, to reimpose their control. They were driven by anti-Catholicism and a fear of the political instability James' policies were creating. It could be argued that the revolution was an extension of the Exclusion Crisis and that the fear of a Catholic succession from 1668 was the dominant theme for the later Stuarts for the next 20 years.

> This paragraph focuses on the main theme of the question with some good detail and clear comment on how exclusion led to political division and instability.

> The second part of the paragraph needs to be more explicit in indicating how it is addressing the theme of anti-Catholicism and political instability.

> This conclusion stresses the focus of the argument, but it could be broader in line with the wording of question.

Key issues relevant to the question are explored, although treatment of the issues is uneven. Some of the evaluations are only partly substantiated. This essay needs more shaping to the specific wording and concepts of the question. This could be done by using the key words of the question more. There is also scope, in places, for developing the depth of support to further illustrate the points the author is trying to make.

Moving from a Level 4 to Level 5

This essay achieves a Level 4. Read the essay again and the comments provided. Make a list of the additional features required to push a Level 4 essay into Level 5.

AS-level questions

To what extent were religious divisions the main reason for the failure of the republican regimes of the years 1649 to 1660?

Were divisions over religion the main reason for Charles II's difficulties with his parliaments in the years 1660 to 1681?

3 Social and intellectual change, 1625–88

Population growth

Reasons for the increase in population

The changes in England's population during the seventeenth century are outlined in the table below:

Year	Population (millions)
1625	4.1
1656	5.3
1688	4.8

There were a number of reasons for the rising population:
- The country had enjoyed domestic peace since 1485 and the end of the Wars of the Roses. In the sixteenth century the population rose from 3 million to 4 million, and the trend continued during the first half of the seventeenth century.
- Changes in agriculture, such as the **enclosure** of land and the growth of areas under cultivation, ensured a stable supply of food for the growing population.
- During the seventeenth century many Protestants migrated from Europe to escape religious persecution.

However, the rise in population size slowed considerably and even declined in the second half of the seventeenth century, due to:
- the large number of deaths during the civil wars
- the Great Plague of 1665, which caused up to 100,000 deaths in London alone
- many non-conformists migrating to America, where they could worship freely
- marriage often being delayed until people were in their late twenties, which reduced the average size of families.

The impact of population growth on urban development and rural change

In 1625 most people lived in the countryside, and the majority of the population was concentrated in the south-east of England. This changed during the seventeenth century, as young people moved from some southern parishes, where opportunities were limited, to more open parishes in the Midlands and the north. The enclosure of agricultural land that had begun under the Tudors continued in Stuart England. Fewer people were needed to work the land, which led to depopulation in several areas of southern England. Overpopulation and a limited job market in the countryside and smaller towns made London a magnet for rural migrants.

In 1625, 5.8 per cent of the population lived in towns. Urban and industrial development meant that by the end of the century this figure had risen to 13.3 per cent, of which 11.5 per cent lived in London.

London

London dominated England in terms of population and importance. By 1625 the population of London had risen above 200,000. By 1660 it had doubled again. By 1688 London was home to 500,000 people and was on the verge of becoming the largest city in Europe. The city grew due to its geographical position for trade. It was also significant for many aspects of national life, including:
- government
- finance
- industry
- culture.

London's growth was partly due to people moving there from the rest of England and from Europe.

London was larger than the next 50 English towns put together. The next largest English towns, ranging in population from 10,000 to 30,000, were:
- Norwich, an important centre of the cloth trade
- Bristol, a thriving port
- Newcastle, the hub of a growing coal industry
- York
- Exeter.

Spectrum of importance

Below are a sample exam question and a list of general points which could be used to answer the question. Use your own knowledge and the information on the opposite page to reach a judgement about the importance of these general points to the question posed. Write numbers on the spectrum below to indicate their relative importance.

Having done this, write a brief justification of your placement, explaining why some of these factors are more important than others. The resulting diagram could form the basis of an essay plan.

How far was population increase driven by an increase in food supplies?

1 Food supplies

2 Rates of fertility

3 Rates of mortality

4 English custom of late marriage.

←——————————————————————————————————————→
Least important   Most important

 Eliminate irrelevance

Below are a sample exam question and a paragraph written in answer to this question. Read the paragraph and identify parts of the paragraph that are not directly relevant to the question. Draw a line through the information that is irrelevant and justify your deletions in the margin.

To what extent was the changing size of the population responsible for urban development in the years 1625–88?

Between 1625 and 1688 the population of England rose from 4.1 million to 4.8 million. There were many reasons for this increase, including the increases in food production and the migration from Europe into England by people escaping religious persecution. Most people, around 80 per cent of the population, lived in the countryside and worked in agriculture. There were several large towns such as Norwich and York, but London was the biggest city by far, with a population of over 500,000. Many people left the countryside because of overpopulation and low rates of pay, and moved to London to find work. Some other towns were also growing in size because of the development of local industries, such as coal in Newcastle and cloth in Norwich. Urban development was also caused by the growth of trade. With such a large population, London needed a constant supply of food and other products, which came from all over the country.

Poverty and the Poor Laws

The growth of poverty

The increase in population resulted in **inflation**. Historians draw attention to a century of inflation in the years 1540 to 1640, as the population increase put pressure on resources, particularly food. Prices increased by as much as 800 per cent but wages rose by only 300 per cent. As a result, there was an increase in the levels of poverty, and a growing division between rich and poor.

Those particularly affected were the people that did not produce enough food themselves to feed their own family and therefore did not have any left to sell. The growing proportion of the population who were increasingly reliant on wage labour also saw a decline in their living standards. Agriculture relied on seasonal employment, and many rural labourers could only find employment for six months of the year. Furthermore, with a growing population there were more people than there were jobs available. As a result, poverty increased as more people struggled to find full-time employment.

The Poor Laws

In the century before 1640 the population grew faster than the resources of food. There were times of such pressure that starvation and death were a threat for those at the lower end of society.

The 1601 Elizabethan Poor Law established a system which provided basic relief for those unable to work. Although the law set up a legal framework to tackle poverty, there was no further reform of the system until 1834. The growth in poverty was reflected in the rise in the poor rate, from £250,000 per year in 1650 to £700,000 per year by the end of the seventeenth century.

To support the poor, the government attempted to regulate the trade in grain. This was to ensure that in times of harvest failure there were sufficient stocks of grain available at a low price in order to prevent starvation. In response to harvest failures in 1629 and 1630, Charles I's Privy Council issued new **Books of Orders**. The Books were instructions to Justices of the Peace about how they should carry out their local government duties. The Books included advice on how to levy the poor rate and what actions to take when dealing with the poor. An important innovation was to encourage young people to take up apprenticeships. By 1640, 1,400 officers were responsible for organising poor relief in the parishes.

Beggars and vagrants

In the early 1600s, as a result of a growing population, there was a lot of underemployment. Most people still worked in agriculture, which was a seasonal economy; therefore many did not have work throughout the whole year. During this period there were simply too many people seeking full-time work that was often not available.

Rising unemployment, combined with economic hardship, resulted in an increase in homeless beggars who toured the country. Most of these vagrants were in their late teens or early twenties. Records show that 22 per cent of vagrants that passed through Salisbury in the early modern period had already covered 100 miles by the time they arrived. Begging and vagrancy became more of an issue in times of scarce resources.

Vagrants were seen as sources of crime and instability and were often rounded up and punished. Some vagrants were later transported to American colonies. Laws, such as the 1662 Settlement Law, were passed to limit movement. If a man left his own parish to work elsewhere he had to possess a settlement certificate guaranteeing that his home parish would pay for his return if he needed poor relief.

Mind map

Use the information on the opposite page and your own knowledge to add detail to the mind map below to develop your understanding of social and economic problems in the years 1625–88.

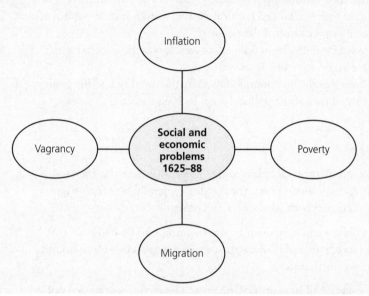

 Develop the detail

Below are a sample exam question and a paragraph written in answer to this question. The paragraph contains a limited amount of detail. Annotate the paragraph to add additional detail to the answer.

How accurate is it to say that poverty decreased over the years 1625 to 1688?

After 1660 there was still widespread poverty. This was despite what could be seen as economic improvements. Poverty varied depending on individual circumstances. After 1660, however, inflation and population change impacted on the scale of poverty.

The changing structure of society

The nobility's place in the political life of the country

- The political class comprised no more than 5 per cent of the population.
- Economic wealth, predominantly based on land ownership, was the root of the influence that the political classes held, which gave them social and political power. Through their control of 70 per cent of the land, the political class controlled the country.
- The majority of the population were excluded from political power. It was the ownership of land which entitled people to have access to political power.
- At the head of the political structure was the monarch, followed by the nobility and the gentry.
- The nobility formed only a very small part of the political elite. In 1633 the English nobility numbered only 122.

The power of the nobility

The power of the nobility was based on their major landholding. Their influence was therefore linked to food prices and rent rates. As large landowners, the nobility generally benefited from the long period of inflation, as this increased both food prices and rents.

By 1688 the power of some of the nobility and upper gentry was beginning to extend from landholding to encompass trade, finance, rent and manufacturing. They established town houses or London residences as well as their country seats.

It was not always the case that the nobility had large annual incomes. The fortunes of several noble families had declined over time, with some having an annual income of as little as £200 a year.

Under the Tudors the nobility had enjoyed substantial political power which was unchallenged by other social classes. However, in the years 1625–88 there was a gradual decline in their power:

- Noble economic power was being challenged by the new commercial and merchant class in London and provincial towns.
- Most of the nobility sided with the king during the civil war. As a result, many lost money and lands which were confiscated by the republic.
- The victorious republicans abolished the House of Lords in 1649, and it was only revived with the Convention Parliament of 1660.

The changing gentry class

The gentry were a significant group within the political elite. Most of the gentry were substantial landowners, but there were also newer groups such as lawyers and merchants whose wealth was based on non-landed income. Other professionals who could be listed under the non-landed gentry included:

- doctors
- the clergy
- musicians
- architects.

Over time, many of these professionals used their acquired wealth to purchase land for their families to become part of the landed gentry.

In the years 1625–88 the gentry became the largest social group attending universities and the Inns of Court, where they studied law. As they became more educated, especially in farming techniques, they began to farm themselves and worked to improve the quality of their land, notably through drainage and land reclamation. They were keen to maximise their profits from the land and to use their increased income for investment in industries and trading concerns.

Under the Stuarts, the gentry class as a whole enhanced their social standing, personal wealth and educational attainment. This enhanced their political self-confidence, which was reflected in the fact that a number of leading parliamentarians, such as Hampden, Pym and Cromwell, were all drawn from the gentry.

The flaw in the argument

Below are a sample exam question and a paragraph written in answer to this question. The paragraph contains an argument which attempts to answer the question. However, there is an error in the argument. Use your knowledge of this topic to identify the flaw in the argument.

To what extent did the power of the nobility decline in the years 1625–88?

As major owners of land, the nobility dominated society in 1625. However, by 1688 they ceased to do so. Through their ownership of land the nobility held influence and dominated parliament and the governments of all monarchs of the period. The Glorious Revolution of 1688, and the financial revolution that came with it, saw a further shift to the professional classes, as government now became more recognisably that of a modern state. The Glorious Revolution changed the position of the landed elite.

Developing an argument

Below are a sample exam question, a list of key points to be made in the essay and a paragraph from the essay. Read the question, the plan and the sample paragraph. Rewrite the paragraph in order to develop an argument. Your paragraph should answer the question directly, and set out the evidence that supports your argument. Crucially, it should develop an argument by setting out a general answer to the question and reasons that support this.

How accurate is it to say that economic change brought change to the gentry class in the years 1625–88?

Key points:
- Impact of economic change
- Development of professions
- Change in land ownership
- Development of trade.

Sample paragraph:

The gentry class made up the bulk of the Political Nation and thereby held political, social and economic influence in the years 1625 to 1688. Parliament was representative of them, not of the whole population. The gentry were well educated and worked hard to improve their landholdings in order to make a profit out of agriculture. Many of the gentry supported parliament during the civil war, which meant that their role in politics grew under the republic.

Urbanisation and the growth of the professional and merchant classes

Urbanisation

The years 1625–88 witnessed increasing levels of urban development. Some towns became centres of distribution of a wider range of goods than was stocked in the local market economies. A growing number of shops were established in towns which sold a wide range of goods, including tobacco, books, textiles and tea.

Urban development therefore became more concentrated in some larger existing market towns. Norwich, for example, grew in size from 10,000 people in 1550 to over 30,000 in 1650, largely because of its importance as a centre of the cloth trade. The proportion of the population living in towns with a population over 10,000 rose during this period. New urban areas such as Manchester, Sheffield, Derby and Newcastle began to emerge through the amalgamation of industrialised parishes. However, in 1688 the most populous 20 towns were the same as in 1625. Most of these towns were close to the sea or to navigable rivers, which allowed for the easy movement of goods.

The growth of the professional and merchant classes

Urban growth and the emergence of shops also brought the development of the professions and merchant classes. Service and leisure activities developed as part of this urban development, to cater for and exploit the urban market. Lawyers, doctors and estate agents had a larger client base in urban centres.

In Stuart England a high proportion of sons of the gentry studied at the Inns of Court in London, and had at least some form of legal training in order to meet the demands of landowning. Such widespread legal knowledge meant that early modern England was an extremely litigious society. By 1625 there were proportionally as many lawyers as there are now.

Other structural changes to the economy also brought about the greater emergence of the professions. As England increasingly competed with the Dutch and the French after 1660, there was a necessary development of administration. War and trade demanded more services from doctors, lawyers, financiers, teachers and architects.

The years 1625–88 saw the growth of a merchant class involved in overseas trade. The East India Company was a very profitable enterprise trading in cotton, silk, tea and spices. It grew in importance under Charles II, who allowed the company to acquire territory in India in order to protect its trading interests. A growing number of London merchants became very rich on the proceeds of Indian trade. Other merchants were involved in the profitable sugar and tobacco trade with America.

Simple essay style

Below is a sample essay question. Use your own knowledge and the information on the opposite page to produce a plan for this question. Choose four general points, and provide three pieces of specific information to support each general point.

Once you have planned your essay, write the introduction and conclusion for the essay. The introduction should list the points to be discussed in the essay. The conclusion should summarise the key points and justify which point was the most significant.

How accurate is it to say that the expansion of overseas trade in the years 1625–88 was responsible for the growth of the professional and merchant classes?

 ## Mind map

Use the information on the opposite page to add detail to the mind map below.

The status of women

Seventeenth-century Britain was very much a **patriarchal** and misogynist society. This was justified by the Bible and its negative portrayals of women. Due to the original sin of Eve, women in the early modern period were regarded as weak and open to temptation. Medical theories explained and justified the biblical view of women as inferior. It was argued not only that they were physically weaker than men but that their brains were different, making them intellectually inferior and virtually incapable of being educated. The proper role for women was seen as being married, looking after the home and the children, and being meek and submissive to their husbands.

There was no significant change in the status of women in the period 1625–88. In Stuart England women were excluded from education, the professions and many aspects of society. Women's roles were defined by their relationship to the men in their life – their fathers or husbands.

The impact of wealth on the status of women

As with men, women towards the top of society were in a better position than the majority of the population. Women could have social, economic and political influence in line with their economic standing. Some wives of landowners, for example, acted as estate managers alongside their husbands. Some wives of farmers, labourers and craftsmen took a role in the family economy. Despite this, there were limits to how they could wield their influence. Women could not hold any of the formal offices through which the political class exercised control. Despite the recent example of the reign of Elizabeth I and other notable strong female role models, such as Bess of Hardwick, women had to exercise their influence in less open political forums.

The impact of the revolutionary years, 1640–60

The revolutionary years from 1640 to 1660 provided the most opportunities for women to subvert the norms. During the civil war, women contributed to the war effort, preached, prophesised and published. However, although the civil war created opportunities for women, the extent of the transformation of women's roles should not be overemphasised.

The war effort

Some women took over the management of estates during their husband's absence as they fought in the civil war. Women also became garrison commanders when their houses were besieged. In London, women worked on building fortifications and tended to the wounded.

Religion

Following the breakdown of governmental control over religious practice in the 1640s, women were able to play a significant role in certain religious movements, such as the Levellers and Quakers, which questioned society's norms. Quakers, for example, believed that the crucifixion had spiritually redeemed women from their subjugation to men.

The civil war also witnessed an upsurge in female prophets. It is estimated there were 300 women prophets during the 1640s and 1650s. It can be argued that through the role of prophets women gained a degree of authority and were able to make their voices heard.

Petitions and popular politics

Petitions gave women a voice denied to them in formal politics. Women petitioned for peace, freedom of trade, changes to the imprisonment laws as well as other political issues.

In August 1643 a crowd of women petitioned parliament for peace and food and in 1649 10,000 women presented another petition to parliament, to release John Lilburne (see page 52).

Writing

The collapse of censorship enabled women to publish their ideas and thoughts. There was an enormous increase in the number of publications by women.

The impact of the Restoration

In 1660 Charles II reimposed on women the order of pre-war times. However, there remained some notable examples of women who broke through the limits of male-dominated society. For example, Bridget Bendish, the granddaughter of Oliver Cromwell and daughter of the New Model Army general Henry Ireton, managed a saltpan and refinery in East Anglia in the Restoration period and challenged to a duel a man who insulted her grandfather. Yet, by 1688 men continued to control society.

Support or challenge?

Below is a sample exam question which asks how far you agree with a specific statement. Below this are a series of general statements which are relevant to the question. Using your own knowledge and the information on the opposite page, decide whether these statements support or challenge the statement in the question and tick the appropriate box.

How far do you agree that the status of women improved in the years 1625 to 1688?

	SUPPORT	CHALLENGE
Women could play a key economic role		
Women petitioned parliament		
Women played a prominent role in the Quaker movement		
Women could not hold public offices		
Women had very few property rights		
Economic standing shaped the influence of women		
Early modern Britain was a patriarchal society		

ⓘ Recommended reading

Below is a list of suggested further reading on this topic.

- S. Mendelson and P. Crawford, *Early Modern Women, 1550–1720*, pages 365–430, Oxford University Press (1998)
- A. L. Erickson, *Women and Property: In Early Modern England*, Introduction and Conclusion, Routledge (1995)
- L. Lunger Knoppers, *Cambridge Companion to Early Modern Women's Writing*, Chapter 8, Cambridge University Press (2009)

Radical political ideas, including the Levellers and the Diggers

The breakdown in royal and church authority occasioned by civil war and revolution facilitated the development of radical political ideas and movements. Two of the most notable were the Levellers and the Diggers.

The Levellers

- The Levellers were a predominantly London-based pressure group that sought political, economic and social reform.
- They developed as a result of economic distress caused by the civil war.
- The Levellers attacked kingly authority and **kingship** from the beginning of the movement in 1646.
- The movement had little time for Charles I and wanted to replace kingship with a government dominated by a representative of the people.
- The leading figure in the movement was John Lilburne.

The failure of the Levellers

If the Levellers were to stand any chance of success they would need more support in the New Model Army. As division threatened the army, it held the Putney Debates in October 1647 to discuss with the Levellers their written constitution, the Agreement of the People, and particularly their ideas on the extension of the franchise.

The short-term pragmatic alliance between the Levellers and the army leadership collapsed before the **regicide**. In March 1649 the leading Levellers, including Lilburne, were arrested. However, the Levellers continued their propaganda war against the Rump and the army. In the pamphlet, *The Hunting of the Foxes* (1649), Cromwell, in particular, was attacked. The Levellers' Third Agreement was an attempt to inspire army mutiny. The response was limited and quickly crushed by Cromwell at Burford in May 1649.

It was not only the determination of the Rump and the army leadership to quell the Levellers that limited the movement, but also the fact that the Rump had money to pay the army. This prevented unrest among the troops and limited Leveller influence and the threat they posed.

The failure of the Levellers was also rooted in their alienation of those towards the bottom of society through:

- social reforms being too limited
- economic reforms being too limited
- those without property not being included in plans for extension of the franchise.

The Diggers

The Diggers were a reaction to the political upheavals of the years 1647 to 1649, as parliament struggled without success to negotiate a peaceful settlement with Charles I. They grew in importance after the king's execution in 1649. Led by Gerard Winstanley, the Diggers established a community outside London as a proposed solution to social inequalities. The ideas and actions of the Diggers offered a fundamental challenge to the nature of politics and society at the time, but their influence was limited. Unlike the Levellers, the Diggers believed in total social and political equality. They referred to themselves as the True Levellers.

The failure of the Diggers

The ultimate failure of the Diggers was due to the hostility of those who owned the land around their community at St George's Hill. After a year of continued hostility the Digger community collapsed.

Other Digger communities had been set up throughout England in Northamptonshire, Kent, Buckinghamshire, Hertfordshire, Middlesex, Bedfordshire, Leicestershire, Gloucestershire and Nottinghamshire, but none of them survived. Despite their immediate failure, the significance of the Diggers was the path they laid for future radicals, based on the following central ideas:

- Direct Action – the Diggers provided an example of taking action in politics rather than just relying on their ideas.
- Communism – in the establishment of their communes, the Diggers provided an example of Communism in action.
- Liberation theology – the ideas of the Diggers pre-figured radical Christian movements such as those in Latin America in the 1950s and 1960s led by Gustavo Gutierrez of Peru, Leonardo Boff of Brazil, and Jon Sobrino of Spain. This movement aimed to liberate people from poverty and injustice.
- Environmentalism – in living off nature in their communes, the Diggers can be seen as prefiguring the environmental movement.

🔆 Identify the concept

Below are five sample exam questions based on some of the following concepts:

- **Cause** – questions concern the reasons for something, or why something happened
- **Consequence** – questions concern the impact of an event, an action or a policy
- **Change/continuity** – questions ask you to investigate the extent to which things changed or stayed the same
- **Similarity/difference** – questions ask you to investigate the extent to which two events, actions or policies were similar
- **Significance** – questions concern the importance of an event, an action or a policy.

Read each of the questions and work out which of the concepts they are based on.

How accurate is it to say that the Levellers made little impact on government in the years 1645 to 1660?

How far were the Leveller and Digger movements similar to each other in their ideas, organisation and impact in the years 1645 to 1660?

How accurate is it to say that Leveller ideas were primarily focused on economic issues?

How accurate is it to say that the failure to win over the New Model Army in the years 1645 to 1660 was the most important reason for the failure of the Leveller movement?

'The Leveller and Digger movements were fundamentally weakened by their own radicalism.' How far do you agree with this statement?

ℹ️ Recommended reading

Below is a list of suggested further reading on this topic.

- G.E. Aylmer (ed.), *The Levellers in the English Revolution*, pages 9–55, Thames and Hudson (1975)
- A. Sharp (ed.), *The English Levellers*, pages vii–xxii, Cambridge University Press (1998)
- C. Hill, *The World Turned Upside Down*, Chapter 7, Penguin (1972)
- J. Gurney, *Brave Community: The Digger Movement in the English Revolution*, Chapter 5 Manchester University Press, (2007)

Hobbes and Locke: the end of divine right monarchy and a confessional state

REVISED

Thomas Hobbes

Born in 1588, **Thomas Hobbes** had been closely associated with **Francis Bacon** and, while travelling, met the Italian astronomer Galileo. Hobbes wrote about mathematics and science but he is best known for his philosophical works. Hobbes left England in 1640 and lived in Paris until 1652. In 1651 he produced his best known work, *Leviathan*. Hobbes' work questioned the **divine right** of kings by arguing that the right to rule was not granted by God but through a social contract, unwritten or written. According to Hobbes, power was granted by the people, and monarchs could therefore be removed if they broke this contract. The final section of *Leviathan* was a justification of submission to England's new republican regime. Hobbes argued that as Charles I could not protect the English people they were compelled to obey the new state. Furthermore, the new republican state had as much authority as monarchy. Hobbes also put forward the idea of absolute sovereignty whereby a state was legitimised if it could protect the people under its power.

Restoration and the Glorious Revolution

The Restoration saw the reimposition of the monarchy and the idea of divine right monarchy and a confessional state. During the European **Reformation** and the Catholic Counter-Reformation many countries had become confessional states. They adopted either Catholicism or Protestantism as the state religion, and imposed it on the entire population. The Glorious Revolution of 1688 finally undermined divine right monarchy and the confessional state, as William III and Mary II agreed to rule in accordance with the laws of parliament.

In religion, there was a broadening of comprehension that brought an end to the confessional Anglican Church which was reimposed at the Restoration. The Toleration Act of 1689 exempted dissenters from the penal laws if they took an oath of allegiance. Catholicism remained outlawed and England remains formally a Protestant country, with the monarch as head of state and also head of the Protestant state church.

John Locke

John Locke spent much of the 1670s and 1680s on the Continent, only returning to England in 1689 after the Glorious Revolution. It was only at this point that Locke's most famous work, *Two Treatises of Government*, was finally published, albeit anonymously.

Although published after 1688, Locke's *Two Treatises of Government* should be seen in the context of politics pre-1688 and fear of the growing power of Charles II and James II. It was written as an anti-absolutist response to Filmer's *Patriarcha* (1680) which supported the divine right of kings.

Locke focused on the following in support of the argument for exclusion, and this was also used for resistance to the Catholic James II:
- Contractual theory of government – a contract was in place between the monarch and people to prevent absolutism.
- Equality of man – all men deserved to be treated equally, no matter their status.
- Popular sovereignty – power was held by the people.
- The law of nature – certain rights and values were inherently set by nature, meaning that a monarch could not be absolutist.
- Right of resistance – people had the right to resist a monarch acting tyrannically.

Locke's work produced little reaction at the time, and it only became more widely read in the eighteenth century. His theories acquired new significance and more readers as a result of America's struggle for independence in the 1770s.

Quick quizzes at **www.hoddereducation.co.uk/myrevisionnotes**

Identify key terms

Below is a sample exam-style question which includes a key word or term. Key terms are important because their meaning can be helpful in structuring your answer, developing an argument, and establishing criteria that will help form the basis of a judgement.

> How accurate is it to say that the writings of Hobbes and Locke undermined monarchy?

- First, identify the key word or term. This will be a word or phrase that is important to the meaning of the question. Underline the word or phrase.
- Second, define the key word or term. Your definition should set out the key features of the phrase or word that you are defining.
- Third, make an essay plan that reflects your definition.
- Finally, write a sentence answering the question that refers back to the definition.

Now repeat the task, and consider how the change in key terms affects the structure, argument and final judgement of your essay.

> How accurate is it to say that divine right was undermined by the writings of Hobbes and Locke?

 Recommended reading

Below is a list of suggested further reading on the ideas of Hobbes and Locke:

- R. Tuck, *Hobbes: A Very Short Introduction*, Oxford University Press (2002)
- J. Dunn, *Locke: A Very Short Introduction*, Oxford University Press (2003)
- R. Tuck, *Philosophy and Government, 1572–1651*, Chapter 7, Cambridge University Press (1993)
- P. Strathern, *Locke in 90 Minutes*, Constable (1996)

The Scientific Revolution and the Royal Society

The Scientific Revolution

The Renaissance focused on rediscovering the achievements of the ancient world. By the 1600s there was more focus on a scientific approach to knowledge, and the work of the astronomer Copernicus and anatomist Vesalius sparked a new period called the Scientific Revolution.

The following individuals were key to this scientific approach:
- Galileo (1564–1642) – Italian astronomer, physicist, engineer, philosopher and mathematician.
- William Harvey (1578–1657) – English physician who was the first to describe accurately how blood was pumped around the body by the heart. He published his findings in 1628.
- Robert Boyle (1627–91) – Natural philosopher, chemist, physicist and inventor.
- Robert Hooke (1635–1703) – Natural philosopher, inventor and architect. His *Micrographia* (1665), which contained fascinating pictures and instructions on how to use a microscope more effectively, encouraged more people to buy a microscope.
- Isaac Newton (1643–1727) – Physicist and mathematician who is still regarded as one of the most influential scientists of all time.

The essential idea of the Scientific Revolution was that scientific knowledge builds upon itself. Therefore, knowledge and scientific understanding advance steadily and cumulatively to make possible new laws and inventions. From this, scientists like Francis Bacon (1561–1626) argued that 'knowledge is power'.

Francis Bacon and the experimental method

Francis Bacon, through arguing that scientific knowledge should be based on observation, is often viewed as the founder of **empiricism**. Bacon argued that a sceptical and methodical approach should be adopted as part of scientific observation. Bacon's lasting legacy is his approach to experimental method. He influenced leading scientists of the 1650s such as Thomas Browne (1605–82) and the founders of the Royal Society.

The significance of the Royal Society

Historians have shown how important the 1640s and 1650s were in the history of science and its acceptance by intellectual society. There was a great deal of overlap, in terms of personalities and discussion of ideas, between the numerous informal meetings of scientists in the 1650s and the formal royal charter given to the Royal Society in 1662.

The Royal Society's membership derived from the elite and professional class, indicating the acceptance of science among the political class. In order to attract members and funding, the meetings of the Society became a place for public demonstration of exciting science.

The Society's journal, *Philosophical Transactions*, which appeared in 1665, was the world's first scientific journal. Owned by Henry Oldenburg, the Society's first Secretary, it was designed to publicise discoveries and build support among the elite. Published monthly, it recorded new ideas and demonstrations and included letters from scientists around the world.

The importance that was attached to science in the years 1660 to 1688 can be seen in the prominence of the key scientists of the period: Isaac Newton, Robert Boyle and Robert Hooke. Charles II's amateur interest in science (he had studied mathematics and set up a chemical laboratory in his chambers at Whitehall) and his support for the Royal Society made an impression on fashionable society, even if they did not understand many of the new discoveries. That Newton is still so well known today reflects the scale of his achievements.

Establish criteria

Below is a sample exam question which requires you to make a judgement. The key term in the question has been underlined. Defining the meaning of the key term can help you establish criteria that you can use to make a judgement.

Read the question, define the key term and then set out two or three criteria based on the key term, which you can use to reach and justify a judgement.

How significant was the work of philosophers and scientists in <u>changing ideas</u> in the years 1625 to 1688?

Definition:

_____

_____

Criteria to judge the extent of the significance of the work of philosophers and scientists in changing ideas in the period 1625–88:

_____

_____

_____

_____

Reach a judgement

Having defined the key term and established a series of criteria, you should now make a judgement. Consider how significant the work of philosophers and scientists was in changing ideas in the years 1625 to 1688 according to each criterion. Summarise your judgements below:

Criterion 1:

_____

Criterion 2:

_____

Criterion 3:

_____

Finally, sum up your judgement. Based on the criteria, how significant was the work of philosophers and scientists in changing ideas in the years 1625 to 1688?

_____

_____

_____

Tip: Remember that you should weigh up evidence of the extent of the significance in your conclusion.

Exam focus

Below is a model answer to an exam-style question. Read it and the comments around it.

How far were religious radicals responsible for the political instability of the years 1648 to 1660?

In the years 1648 to 1660, due to the collapse of royal authority and the revolution, there was an explosion of radical ideas and the emergence of new groups to promote them, such as the Levellers and the Diggers. Radical ideas served to both influence government policy and cause the government to react against these groups. However, political instability had a number of other root causes, including the natural conservatism of the MPs in the Rump and Protectorate parliaments and the recurring threat of royalism.

In 1648 millenarianism was the driving religious and political radical idea that made New Model Army officers, including Cromwell, Ireton and Harrison, consider the execution of a divine right monarch sanctioned by God. Their providential thinking derived from the millenarian idea that they needed to prepare for Christ's second coming. These ideas were put forward by the Fifth Monarchists, one of the few radical groups to survive the years of the Republic. In order to prepare for Christ's arrival, the execution of Charles I as the 'man of blood' was necessary. While it could be argued that Charles' actions had made it politically necessary to remove him, it was millenarian radical ideas that allowed the regicides to justify such a unique and radical step in January 1649. The significance of radical ideas can clearly be seen as leading to the regicide and also the consequent political instability from division over how settlement without monarchy after 1649 could be achieved. The ideas of the Fifth Monarchists were also significant when Cromwell dissolved the Rump in 1653 and replaced it with the Nominated Assembly. This 'Parliament of Saints' was designed to fulfil the aims of the Fifth Monarchists, who believed that a number of 'saints' should rule the earth in preparation for Christ's second coming.

It was out of the civil war, the armies of parliament and the failure of settlement with Charles I that radical groups promoting radical political ideas, like the Levellers, emerged. The development of the Leveller movement was the result of economic distress caused by civil war, especially in London, in a time of political and religious uncertainty. As a reaction to this, and building on an intellectual tradition of dissent and ideas of natural law and traditional English freedoms, the Levellers called for economic, political and religious reform. The Levellers created political instability by dividing the army and alienating the political elite. After the regicide, the crushing of the Leveller mutiny at Burford in May 1649 indicated that the New Model Army officers had no intention of letting the Levellers seize the political initiative at their expense. The Rump Parliament passed legislation to clamp down on the Levellers and the movement had effectively ended by the end of 1649.

The spread of radical ideas due to the freedom of these years meant that many groups developed from similar, earlier ideas or other radical movements. The Diggers – or, as they styled themselves, the True Levellers – clearly had some links with the Leveller movement, but were more influenced by the personality of one leading figure, Gerard Winstanley. Unlike the Levellers, the Diggers' radical political ideas meant they believed in total social and political equality. The Diggers established a commune outside London and saw such organisations as a solution to social inequalities. In the eyes of the political elite, the Diggers were another example of the army and revolution having created political instability by undermining the order of the pre-civil war years. The movement was no longer a force by 1651 and legislation such as the Blasphemy Act of 1650 severely restricted the activities of radical groups.

A strong introduction that deals with the specific wording of the question but also shows conceptual understanding. The introduction makes a clear argument and introduces other factors not mentioned in the question.

This paragraph deals with 1648 and therefore the starting point of the essay question. It also shows the importance of millenarianism and illustrates how this had an impact later.

Within this paragraph a key group are dealt with very efficiently showing an appreciation that radicalism is not just religious.

Again, this paragraph shows a range of knowledge but also good organisation in dealing with the Diggers directly after the Levellers, thereby linking the two in terms of the development of radical ideas in the period.

In reality, it could be argued that neither the Levellers' nor the Diggers' radical political ideas really had a significant impact on the political direction of the years 1648 to 1660. Another important reason for political instability was the natural conservatism of the government and parliament. A link can be drawn here between the actions of the radical groups and this conservatism, because it could be argued that the Adultery and Blasphemy Acts would not have been passed if it was not for the actions of radical groups. Also, the legal reform recommended would not have been rejected by the Rump if the Levellers and others had not pushed for such reform. The conservatism of government is also evident under the Nominated Assembly. Although radicals became infamous for their outspoken nature, the majority of members were from the top 5 per cent of the population, and the fact that they failed to abolish tithes or make significant reform demonstrates their lack of desire for change. The fact that the Political Nation almost universally approved of Cromwell's appointment as Lord Protector in 1653 again demonstrates this conservatism, and the fact that there was a property qualification to vote for the First Protectorate Parliament shows that the authorities were not interested in distributing power to those outside the traditional ruling elite.

An alternative reason – the conservatism of the government – for the lack of political stability is explored here. A good link is also made between the actions of the radical groups and the resulting conservatism of the authorities.

Another reason for the lack of political stability and regular changes in government in these years was the threat of royalism. The Rump Parliament itself was created in order to carry out the trial of Charles I, and Cromwell's invasion of Ireland was also triggered by the continuing threat of royalists there. The need for a large standing army in these years was also necessitated by this threat, and when the future Charles II invaded in 1651, triggering the Third Civil War, the threat was as heightened as ever. In 1655 Cromwell resorted to military rule of the country through the Major-Generals, dividing the country into eleven districts, each ruled by a military commander. The Major-Generals varied in their levels of success, and the experiment ended after less than a year, but it is clear that government would have been more stable if the threat of royalism had been extinguished earlier.

Again, precise illustration but also judgement about how important the threat of a royalism was.

In conclusion, it is clear that the spread of religious radicalism meant that the governments of 1648–60 had to change their policies regularly in order to deal with the threat. An equally important threat, however, was that of royalism. Despite the fact that Charles I had died in 1649, his son was evidently popular enough to mount a serious threat to the Republican regime and also had support in Ireland. The threat of both royalism and religious radicalism was heightened by the fact that all governments in these years were made up of a gentry class that was naturally cautious and conservative, and were never interested in expanding the voting franchise or allowing alternative ideas to flourish. Therefore, the natural conservatism of parliament is the most important reason for the lack of political stability.

A well-argued and clear conclusion that comes to a judgement based on an assessment of all the evidence presented in the essay.

This is a good essay, as it focuses and comments on the key words and concepts of the question. However, another reason for the lack of political stability – such as the role of Cromwell or lack of financial stability – could be included.

Using key words

There is a lot of detail on radical ideas. Go through the essay and underline every mention of the words 'radical ideas'. Next, look at an essay you have written and underline your use of key words. Can you improve on your own efforts in the light of what you have seen here?

AS-level questions

How significant was population change for the English economy in the years 1625 to 1688?

How far did English society change in the years 1625–88?

4 Economy, trade and empire, 1625–88

Agriculture

Capital investment in agriculture

Early in the seventeenth century, the population rise and consequent surplus labour meant that landowners could increase productivity through deployment of additional labour. Extra demand for food resources also made farming more profitable for landowners. However, population stagnation after 1656 reduced the size of the labour market and led to a general rise in wages. Consequently, landowners looked at better exploitation of existing land through capital investment in order to increase productivity. In many parts of Britain woodlands were cleared and converted to pasture. The most extensive land clearance took place in the fenlands of East Anglia, where 4,000 Dutch drainage experts were employed to bring the land under cultivation.

Changes in agricultural techniques

Population stagnation in the mid-seventeenth century drove some farmers to become more efficient by exploring new techniques, along with new crops that offered better profits. Improved agricultural techniques included:

- floating water meadows to enhance grazing – each year meadows were flooded with a few centimetres of water to protect the land from frosts and thus increase grass crops
- improved drainage
- better rotation of crops
- use of root crops such as potatoes, carrots and turnips
- improvements to farm equipment
- selective breeding of livestock
- an increase in the amount of land farmed
- more extensive use of manure
- more extensive use of fertilisers
- introduction of new ideas and techniques from the Netherlands.

For example, the use of turnips as a fodder crop and clover as a new breed of grass helped overcome the shortage of fertilisers and animal manure. These two crops could be stored for winter animal feed, and their introduction in East Anglia turned areas of heath and chalk into land suitable for grain. These changes enabled farmers to maintain large numbers of animals throughout the year.

From 1670, as a result of changes in agriculture, England ceased to be a net importer of grain and became an exporter.

Specialised farming

The growth of urban employment required the development of specialised farming to increase production with less farm labour.

The development of specialised farming through enclosure, the growth of a wider range of crops, the establishment of larger, more commercial farms and the use of new techniques, particularly from the Netherlands, did not happen on a systematic basis. There was no agricultural revolution in the 1600s, but the agrarian economy became more efficient.

The growth of London increased demand and spurred a more specialised regional farming and commercialisation that helped develop a national market.

Regional specialisation was part of an emerging national market and was linked to the geography and climate of England. In general, the north and west (highland) focused on pastoral farming whereas the south and east (lowland) focused on arable farming. Within this, however, there was further specialisation based on local climate or soil. For example, north-west Norfolk was arable while the south-east was wood pasture.

Mind map

Construct a mind map to illustrate the range of factors that contributed to **changes** and **development** in farming across the century.

 Spot the mistake a

Below are a sample exam question and a paragraph written in answer to this question. Why does this paragraph not get into Level 4? Once you have identified the mistake, rewrite the paragraph so that it displays the qualities of Level 4. The mark scheme on page 94 will help you.

How far was agriculture transformed in the years 1625–88?

There was an agricultural revolution in the seventeenth century. This happened predominantly not so much because of new techniques but because of the impact of new ideas and crops. The role of finance and the reorganisation of farmland also had a significant impact. Thus, even though the population expanded even more after 1650 the revolution in farming enabled this growing population to be fed more efficiently. Poverty and starvation were unheard of by 1700.

The development of national markets and the cloth trade REVISED

National markets

In 1625 Britain had not established a single national economy. Difficulties with communications, coupled with the absence of strong commercial enterprises, meant that regional economic activity was centred around market towns where local produce and livestock were bought and sold. Industrial activity was also regional, linked to areas where raw materials were easily accessible. Manufacturing of goods was not carried out in factories, but in houses or outbuildings in rural areas.

It was only gradually, over the years 1625 to 1688, that a broader, more national economy and market emerged. By 1688 this development had been facilitated in the following ways:

- Better communication – the navigability of many rivers was improved, allowing for the speedier movement of goods.
- Specialisation – as communication improved many regions developed local specialities. Wiltshire, for example, became a centre for cheese making, and its products were sold throughout Britain.
- Finance – As a national economy began to take shape, a more sophisticated financial structure began to emerge with the development of banks and other financial institutions.
- Urban development – In 1625 goods could only be bought from the markets in different towns. By 1688 shops had sprung up throughout the country, offering a wide range of goods to supply a growing consumer market.

However, the creation of a national market and a unified economy was essentially limited to England and Wales. Scotland did not gain a share in the new markets. Her agricultural land was not as productive as England's, and transport links between England and Scotland were not well developed. Additionally, most English politicians showed no interest in Ireland at all. Ireland had a separate culture based on language and religion, and so the country was treated more as a colonial possession than as an equal with England and Scotland.

The cloth trade

Textiles, or the cloth trade, was by far the largest manufacturing concern, employing approximately 200,000 workers, predominantly in the south-west, the Pennines and East Anglia. The cloth trade had both a national and an international market. One reason for the prominence of the cloth trade was that the whole sequence of manufacture could be split up into separate processes. This led to a greater division of labour, which lowered costs and raised productivity. It also fitted with family structure, with all members having specified roles. Throughout this period the textile industry spread outside the initial centres of Norwich and Colchester and became established in Manchester and the north-west of England.

The changing 'new draperies' and the impact of Protestant refugees

The staple of the English textile trade before the mid-sixteenth century was woollen broadcloth, known as the 'old draperies'. The 'new draperies', introduced in the 1560s by Dutch immigrants, were lighter than the old wool-based materials. The new draperies revived the English textile market. Norwich and Colchester had strong trading links with the Netherlands. Dutch trade helped to establish East Anglia as a major centre for the new draperies.

Louis XIV revoked the protection given to Protestants in France under the Edict of Nantes. In doing so he signalled that he would start to persecute French Protestants. From the 1650s a growing number of Dutch and French Protestants migrated to England to avoid religious persecution. These skilled workers helped in the development of lighter fabrics, including silk, which was blended with English wool. The introduction of the smaller Dutch loom also helped develop the new draperies. This allowed the production of more delicate items, precisely at the time when Italian and French fashions that were more intricate were becoming more popular.

Complete the paragraph

Below are a sample exam question and a paragraph written in answer to this question. The paragraph contains a point and specific examples, but lacks a concluding analytical link back to the question. Complete the paragraph, adding this link in the space provided.

How far did the development of the new draperies in the years 1625–88 have a significant social and economic impact?

The new draperies developed through the impact of European ideas and in particular immigration to areas of England like East Anglia. They had a significant impact on the social and economic life of these areas. Norwich and Colchester, in particular, benefited from the settlement in East Anglia of Protestant refugees from the Netherlands. This happened over a period of time, actually beginning in the sixteenth century. The impact of this immigration can be seen in the development, over time, of the new draperies in these areas. It could be argued that by the end of the seventeenth century the new draperies were actually not new. Furthermore it could also be argued that they were not revolutionary techniques and thus in terms of their economic impact they had a gradual impact.

Overall, ...

_____

_____

Simple essay style

a

Below is a sample exam question. Use your own knowledge and the information on the opposite page to produce a plan for this question. Choose four general points, and provide three pieces of specific information to support each general point.

Once you have planned your essay, write the introduction and conclusion for the essay. The introduction should list the points to be discussed in the essay. The conclusion should summarise the key points and justify which point was the most important.

How significant was the impact of religious refugees in the development of Britain's economy in the years 1625–88?

London, economic development and the growth of banking and insurance

The growth of London and its impact on economic development

The growth of London was one of the major developments of the early modern period. In 1550 London was still essentially a medieval city with a population of 120,000 people. By 1700 London had developed into a metropolitan centre with close to 500,000 inhabitants. London's sheer size meant that it dominated Britain's economy and culture. The next-largest towns, Norwich, Bristol and Newcastle, each had about 20,000 inhabitants. While these towns also grew, Norwich, despite being the second-largest city, had only 30,000 inhabitants by 1688.

Reasons for London's growth

- Deaths outnumbered births in London; therefore migration was the principal reason behind London's population increase.
- London attracted a great number of servants and apprentices.
- Poverty in the countryside encouraged migrants to head to London from all parts of Britain in the hope of finding employment.

Impact on economic development

The expanding population and growth of London stimulated agricultural trade. Urban growth created a surge in agricultural productivity. London's food needs were supplied by a large number of farms, often many miles from the capital. Other goods were supplied by the river trade and, from the 1660s, the new turnpike roads. The coastal trade allowed for goods to come from farther afield, such as coal from Newcastle.

The development of a banking and financial system later in the century further secured London's dominant position in the economic, social, cultural and political life of Britain. Goods passed through London's docks for redirection to other parts of the country. London's development also saw a shift in economic power. Until the 1660s most private wealth was accrued through the ownership of land. By 1688 the growth of banking and financial institutions had created a new class of rich entrepreneurs.

The growth of banking and insurance

This period witnessed the emergence of a more sophisticated system of banking and insurance. Business and commerce needed a credit system that was flexible. The development of credit came from Bills of Exchange that were given in lieu of payment, with interest charged depending on time of repayment. Over time, with the expansion of London and its trade, Bills of Exchange were used to pay off debts instead of cash. From this developed a banking system, as London merchants and goldsmiths accepted the Bills and offered credit to businessmen and others by opening accounts for the deposit or withdrawal of cash. Other provincial centres soon followed suit, leading to the establishment of a national banking system.

There were two forms of banking: private, and business and insurance.

Private banking

This was very limited in the early seventeenth century. There were no private banks outside London and even in London they were only starting to develop by 1688. Family and friends were the source of finance for most people in need, rather than private banking. Private banking developed as a result of the development of business and insurance banking.

Banking services proved invaluable in helping to finance wars and conflicts overseas, especially the Anglo-Dutch wars of the 1660s and 1670s.

Business and insurance

England's emergence as one of the world's leading trading countries further stimulated the banking and insurance sectors. English ships that carried goods all around the world were insured by English banks or by specialist insurance companies. Property insurance also developed, particularly after the Great Fire of London. Other forms of insurance developed after 1660, notably fire insurance. Another development was the increase in **joint stock companies** as British overseas trade expanded. Coffee houses became places where financiers could obtain news about, and deal in, shares and government bonds. The insurance business further reinforced the importance of London in the national economy.

Eliminate irrelevance

Below are a sample exam question and a paragraph written in answer to this question. Read the paragraph and identify parts of the paragraph that are not directly relevant to the question. Draw a line through the information that is irrelevant and justify your deletions in the margin.

How significant were developments in banking in stimulating change in the English economy in the years 1660 to 1688?

Developments in banking were of significance in changing the English economy in the years after 1660, alongside other factors. Key to stimulating change in the English economy was competition with the Dutch. The Second Navigation Act passed by Charles II further focused on positioning England to compete with the Dutch in trade. This competition lay behind Charles II's decision to go to war with the Dutch in the 1660s and 1670s. By the 1680s the English were carrying more trade in direct competition with the Dutch. To help finance competition with the Dutch banking in London developed, in particular through Bills of Exchange. The insurance industry also developed in line with the development of the English carrying trade. As part of the Glorious Revolution of 1688, further developments in the banking system saw a further shift from Dutch to English dominance of merchant trading as England's grip on North America and the Caribbean provided her with key resources to exploit the Atlantic triangular trade. Therefore the development of banking came as part of the shift in the English economy due to its changing relationship with the Dutch.

Spot the mistake

Below are a sample exam question and a paragraph written in answer to this question. Why does this paragraph not get into Level 4? Once you have identified the mistake, rewrite the paragraph so that it displays the qualities of Level 4. The mark scheme on page 94 will help you.

How far do you agree that the British economy in the years 1660–88 was transformed by the development of banking?

The development of banking in the early years of the reign of Charles II was key in transforming the English economy. Banking was developed as a result of the conflict with the Dutch in the 1660s and early 1670s. The conflict with the Dutch was essentially an economic war as England competed for the markets the global Dutch trading empire had been exploiting. To fund this conflict, banking developed.

The impact of imperial expansion

The significance of North America and Jamaica

During the seventeenth century approximately 300,000 people emigrated to North America, the numbers reaching a peak by 1660. Many emigrants established settlements on the east coast, including Virginia, Maryland and New England, as well as in the West Indies.

Most emigrants hoped to achieve a better life. Puritans, who established many settlements in New England, created religious communities where they could worship freely instead of suffering discrimination in England. Catholics also escaped persecution in England by settling in Maryland.

In 1654, following Cromwell's attack on Spain's Caribbean colonies, England secured control of Jamaica. In economic terms the key significance of North America and Jamaica was that over time it allowed Britain to develop control of the triangular trade (see page 68).

The Caribbean was important for its valuable raw materials, notably the staple crops of sugar, tea and tobacco. Sugar was re-exported to Europe to meet a growing demand linked to the increased taste for tea and coffee. Tobacco exports grew at a rapid rate, from approximately 20,000 pounds in weight before 1625 to 1.5 million pounds in 1629 and approximately 20 million pounds by 1688. The development of tobacco and sugar plantations in the southern parts of North America and the Caribbean further focused England's interests in the slave trade.

The Navigation Acts and the development of mercantilism

As the seventeenth century progressed, and as England began to establish itself as a naval power, the country became more involved in acquiring its own markets abroad and controlling trade.

In 1651 the Rump Parliament passed a Navigation Act designed to weaken the influence of Dutch merchants on English trade:
● All goods coming into England had to be carried in English ships or the ships of the exporting country.
● All trade from England's overseas possessions had to use English ships only.

A further Navigation Act of 1660 extended protection of English trade. This **mercantilism** was intended to close colonial markets to foreign competition and allow the expansion of English overseas trade.

In 1625 England imported more goods than it sold abroad, but this situation had been transformed by 1688 as the country re-exported a wide range of colonial goods to Europe. Among its imports, 49 per cent came from the Americas and the Far East, and 31 per cent of these were then re-exported from England. Towards the end of the seventeenth century England was emerging as a leading naval and merchant power, and structures were being put into place which would see the creation of the British Empire in the eighteenth century.

Complete the paragraph

Below are a sample exam question and a paragraph written in answer to this question. The paragraph contains a point and specific examples, but lacks a concluding analytical link back to the question. Complete the paragraph, adding this link in the space provided.

How far was the introduction of the Navigation Acts responsible for the development of English exports in the period 1651–88?

The Navigation Acts from 1651 did lead to the expansion of the market in the American colonies and their dependence on exports from England over the seventeenth century. From virtually nothing in 1600, by 1688 exports from England to the American colonies accounted for 12 per cent of the total of all exports. The exports also covered a diverse range of products from textiles to weapons to luxury goods for the growing elite of farmers in the American colonies, especially those benefiting from the development of the slave and tobacco trade. Overall, by 1688 the Navigation Acts had...

_____

_____

Recommended reading

Below is a list of suggested further reading on this topic.
- C. Hill, *The Century of Revolution 1603–1714*, Chapter 13, Routledge (1961)
- N. Heard, *Stuart Economy and Society*, pages 71–80, Hodder (1995)
- R. Brenner, *Merchants and Revolution*, Chapter 12, Cambridge University Press (1993)
- B. Coward, *A Companion to Stuart Britain*, Chapter 8, Blackwell (2003)

The development of trade overseas

The effects of the Anglo-Dutch commercial rivalry

Before 1650 the Dutch, and specifically the commercial centre of Amsterdam, dominated trade with world markets. After 1649 the Rump Parliament briefly considered a formal union with their fellow Protestant republicans in the Dutch Republic. However, on the back of the 1651 Navigation Act, England went to war with the Dutch. The subsequent conflict, while essentially a stalemate, was the start of a commercial and military struggle that encompassed a further two conflicts as England sought to establish its primacy over the Dutch in world trade. While Cromwell ended the First Dutch War in 1654 there were two more wars with the Dutch in the 1660s and 1670s under Charles II.

In 1688 the Glorious Revolution that brought the Dutch takeover of England actually marked another shift from Dutch to English dominance of world trade and England's emergence as a global power.

The role of the East India Company

The Dutch were also the main trading competition for the English in the Far East. The East India Company was founded in 1600 to try to establish English economic interest in Asia. It eventually was given the right to maintain its own private army to protect its trading interests alongside the fleet it already possessed. The Company established its main bases at Bombay, Madras and Calcutta. It established control of the highly profitable trade in tea and coffee. Before 1640 the Company handled trade worth £100,000 per year. By 1700 it was handling trade worth more than £700, 000.

The East India Company had its charter revoked in 1657 due to concern at the royalist leanings of its governors, and a rival group of merchants were allowed to take over the Company's possessions. In 1660 the Company regained its charter and had its privileges extended by Charles II during the 1660s. It was allowed to issue its own coinage, acquire territories and make war without needing the consent of the British government. The Restoration also strengthened the Company's position because Charles II's marriage to the Portuguese princess, Catherine of Braganza, brought with it as a **dowry** the islands of Bombay, which the king rented to the Company for £10 a year. The Company also became a popular investment for courtiers and the elite.

The significance of British control of the triangular trade

The triangular trade was the movement of slaves from West Africa to the Caribbean or America, and the transport of goods from these regions back to England.

The Navigation Acts enabled the English to challenge, and then to replace, the dominant position which the Dutch held in colonial trade. As England's sea power grew, the development of trade outside Europe, particularly the Caribbean and American colonies, became a larger part of its economy. After 1650 this trade saw the development of provincial ports on the west coast of Britain, notably Bristol, Liverpool and Glasgow. Charles II's Staple Act of 1663 was designed to increase crown income from the colonial trade. In 1672 the Royal Africa Company was established and exploited the power of the royal navy to secure control of much of the West African coast. By the 1680s about 50,000 slaves a year were being transported to the Caribbean and North America from Africa.

RAG – rate the timeline

Below are a sample exam question and a timeline. Read the question, study the timeline and, using three coloured pens, put a red, amber or green star next to the events to show:

- Red: events and policies that have no relevance to the question
- Amber: events and policies that have some significance to the question
- Green: events and policies that are directly relevant to the question.

1 To what extent was England's rivalry with the Dutch in the years 1651 to 1688 the main reason for the development of England's position as a global trading power?

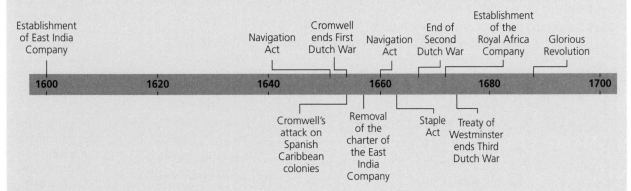

Now repeat the activity with the following questions:

2 How accurate is it to say that England's control of the Caribbean was the main reason for England's growth as a trading power in the years 1650–88?

3 How significant were the Navigation Acts in England's emergence as a trading empire in the years 1651–88?

Below is a sample exam-style essay question and model response. Read it and the comments around it.

How accurate is it to say that there was significant change in agriculture in the years 1625 to 1685?

There was no 'agricultural revolution' in the years 1625 to 1685. Agricultural change was limited, and many of the changes witnessed had already begun before 1625. The change over the period derived from a number of factors. Change can be seen in the increase in specialisation and the increase in productivity. Rather than from a revolution, this came from an adaptation of methods, some of which were linked to the stagnation of the population after 1650.

The majority of agriculture in 1625 was for subsistence purposes, designed for families to be able to meet their own needs rather than for selling to a wider market. Agricultural methods had not changed significantly in centuries. One change across the period was the development of a more commercial market, although this still remained limited. Rather than as a result of an agricultural revolution, this development partly came about as a result of population increase. This population increase was predominantly before 1650 and the levelling off of the population in the latter half of the century eased the pressure on the need for further development of the commercial market. Thus this population stagnation can be seen as important in explaining why there was limited change in agriculture in the post-1650 period. However, the fact that the population did increase meant that farmers had to innovate in order to produce more. Market gardens became more important, especially those near London.

Enclosure was the most obvious sign of agricultural change in response to the need to develop a more commercial form of farming. Enclosure allowed a more intensive use of the land to increase production and the continuing development of this system did stimulate change in production. These larger farms employed labourers who did not have any land of their own, and this further developed the slow process of more landless labourers being employed on the land that, in later centuries, became the norm. Enclosure also brought change to the agricultural economy by moving it more from sheep farming to crop growing in many places. Enclosure became particularly significant after 1660, and protests against the loss of common land became more commonplace. In Buckinghamshire, for example, small farmers who had gradually gained their own land were driven out as a result of enclosure. Despite this change, the methods used on enclosed farms changed little in these years.

The development of larger farms stimulated other changes in agriculture. Larger farms, because of economies of scale, could afford to try new methods. These methods included crop rotation and improvement of fertilisers as well as the introduction of water meadows as a means to flood pastures. Crop rotation was particularly useful as more experimentation could take place. Crops benefiting industry could be invested in, such as flax, hemp and hops. Increased knowledge of agricultural techniques also helped farmers to innovate, and nitrogen-rich crops such as clover and cabbage were used as they helped to fertilise the soil. It was through these incremental changes that bigger change was, eventually, brought to agriculture. However, the majority of smaller farmers were unable to afford to invest in their farms, and small family farms continued to outnumber large 'capital farms'.

This introduction focuses directly on the wording of the question but would benefit from some development.

A paragraph that deals well with the impact of population increase. More detail could be added about what agriculture was like in 1625, to help set up the development of an argument.

This paragraph focuses on how enclosures brought about change, and includes examples of this change.

This is a more focused and supported paragraph, which adds to the argument that agriculture did change as a result of new techniques. It also provides a counter-argument.

Agricultural change was also stimulated by the huge expansion of London and therefore the great demand of a more developed market for food. This also started the development of a more national market for commercial farming and regional specialisation. This increased interest can be illustrated by the Royal Society in 1661 conducting a survey of new farming techniques as a means of aiding improvement in agriculture. However, in some regions, there was little investment and there appears to be a real lack of agricultural change. In Oxfordshire, for example, the same systems and techniques used for the previous 200 years continued to be used, and the county was still able to flourish agriculturally. A national market did not develop in Scotland or Ireland, as transport was inadequate and the government was reluctant to invest heavily in agriculture. Ireland was viewed by the English as a colonial possession with fewer prospects than England, and Scotland's agricultural land was of varied quality.

In conclusion, agriculture certainly changed between 1625 and 1685, and a number of important developments took place which contributed to the wider transformation of the economy. It is clear, however, that this change was not universal, and not all areas of the country and not all classes benefited from these years. Many of the changes were evolutionary rather than revolutionary and had already started before the period, such as the enclosure of common land.

A sound follow-up to the previous paragraph, to take further the importance of the development of London and how this stimulated a different kind of market. It is well balanced because it provides an alternative argument suggesting that this was not entirely beneficial.

A sound conclusion that addresses the question directly, and effectively backs up the original contention found in the introduction with evidence found in the essay.

This is a good essay. It is generally well focused and includes a variety of evidence to support the arguments made. It would benefit from more material that disagrees with the contention in the question (that agriculture changed significantly) to provide more balance.

Extend the range

This essay would achieve a higher mark if it discussed a more extensive range of evidence. Use your own knowledge to write an additional paragraph for this essay.

AS-level questions

How significant were the effects of Anglo-Dutch commercial rivalry in the years 1651–88?

How significant were North America and Jamaica in imperial expansion in the years 1654–88?

Historical interpretations: How revolutionary, in the years to 1701, was the Glorious Revolution of 1688–89?

The significance of revolutionary ideals in the establishment of a constitutional monarchy, Part 1

REVISED

In December 1688, faced with overwhelming opposition to his rule, King James II fled the country and took refuge with Louis XIV of France. A group of about 60 lords and 300 former MPs – Whigs as well as Tories – asked William of Orange to take over the government. On 22 January 1689 the Convention Parliament met to decide how to deal with James' flight. Political opinion was deeply divided.

The Whigs

Whig political theorists had developed revolutionary ideas on the nature of kingship. They claimed that a contract existed between the king and his people which both sides had to uphold. They asserted that James had broken this contract and had exceeded his powers by attempting to establish Catholicism in England. James' actions meant that he had lost the right to rule as king, and that therefore the throne was vacant.

The Tories

Tory beliefs were diametrically opposed to those of the Whigs. They believed in the hereditary succession, and in the divine right of kings to rule over their subjects. Tories had sworn an oath of allegiance to James, and felt they could not break their oath as long as the king lived. They needed some justification for the replacement of James by William of Orange.

The Convention Parliament, 1689

The Convention Parliament formulated a resolution on the monarchy whose wording satisfied most Whigs and Tories:
- James had broken the contract between king and people (Whig).
- He had violated the country's fundamental laws (Whig).
- His flight meant that he had abdicated the throne (Tory).

Tories in the Lords, however, objected to this statement and this led to anti-Tory crowds demonstrating outside parliament. On 3 February 1689 William, in a secret meeting with peers, warned them that he 'would go back to Holland' unless he were made king. William and the political elite agreed that:
- His wife, Mary, would share the title of monarch with William, although without the power.
- If Mary died and William married again, any children from this second marriage would follow Anne (Mary's sister) in the line of succession.

On 6 February this was formally accepted by the Lords and confirmed by the Commons two days later. The throne was offered to William and Mary unconditionally.

Contrasting interpretations

Below are a sample exam question and the extracts referred to in the question. Each extract offers an interpretation of the issue raised by the question. Identify the interpretation offered in each extract and complete the table below, indicating how far the extracts agree with each other, and explaining your answer.

	Extent of agreement	Justification
Extracts 1 and 2		

In the light of differing interpretations, how convincing do you find the view that 1688 was a class revolution?

EXTRACT 1

Adapted from M. Mullett, James II and English Politics 1678–1688 *(1994).*

The role of the governing class and, indeed, of wider social forces should be considered in our reconstruction of what happened in 1688. James II could be seen as a social reformer brought down by entrenched noble and church interests. As part of his policy towards the largely bourgeois dissenters in 1687–88, the king was about to introduce a package of economic reforms in the interest of his new social allies, with a preference for trade over land. This threatened the country's traditional social elite of gentry and nobility. It is highly significant that all the signatories to the invitation to William were either nobles or members of noble houses. Some might see James as brought down essentially by religious attitudes and mass anti-popery, but the experience of this king proves that no seventeenth-century European monarchy was stronger than the landed social and ecclesiastical elite on whose support all government of the day rested and against whose opposition no throne could maintain itself.

EXTRACT 2

Adapted from D. Scott, Leviathan *(2013).*

James II set about building the bureaucratic apparatus of an efficient, centralised state. Determined to make the judiciary and local government subservient to royal authority, he employed professional bureaucrats, answerable to Whitehall, to enforce his will, rather than depending on negotiating consent with local governors. He created a peacetime standing army answerable to him rather than the landed elite. Rights for Catholics and strengthening government were understandable objectives. But attempting both was overambitious and proved impossible without eroding the bedrock of royal support: the Tory-Anglican interest. James could not grasp that the Tories' loyalty to the monarchy was implicitly conditional on him respecting the laws that maintained the Restoration: Anglican ascendancy in Church and State.

Historical interpretations: How revolutionary, in the years to 1701, was the Glorious Revolution of 1688–89?

The significance of revolutionary ideals in the establishment of a constitutional monarchy, Part 2

The Declaration of Rights, 1689

The Declaration of Rights listed all the errors which James had committed, and asserted several traditional liberties of the people. These included:

● Laws could not be suspended without parliament's consent.
● Parliament had to approve all forms of taxation.
● Parliaments should meet frequently.

The Declaration was a compromise document that was left deliberately ambiguous in terms of the constitutional implications of James' removal. There was no statement that James had been resisted, deposed or that he had broken a contract. Similarly, William and Mary were not referred to as 'rightful' or 'lawful' heirs. This meant that those who wished to regard William and Mary as **de facto** monarchs could recognise them as rulers without denying that James was **de jure** king.

A diluted version of the Declaration of Rights passed into law later in 1689, as the Bill of Rights.

William and Mary's coronation

On 13 February 1689, at a formal ceremony at which the Declaration of Rights was read, the crown was offered to William and Mary. On 11 April, at William and Mary's coronation, there was a different coronation oath from that sworn by previous monarchs, indicating their different position and that of parliament:

● Previous oath: to 'confirm to the people of England the laws and customs to them granted by the Kings of England'.
● New oath: 'to govern the people of this kingdom of England, and the dominions thereunto belonging, according to the statutes in Parliament agreed on, and the laws and customs of the same'.

Interpretations of the events of 1688–89

For Whig historians, the Glorious Revolution of 1688–89 brought about fundamental change. The Revolution led to the establishment of a **constitutional monarchy** – one where parliament had much more control over the policies of the monarchy – and the monarchs were expected to get the agreement of the parliament for their actions.

Critics of this Whig interpretation of 1688 do not see the Glorious Revolution as such a decisive break from the previous years. Rather than a revolution, some historians see 1688 as more of a reformation, in that once James was removed, the key aim for the political elite was to bring stability. They did this by the change of monarch.

Others see the Glorious Revolution as confirming the power of the political elite through parliament. The Glorious Revolution and the constitutional changes that followed made clearer the influence of the political elite in parliament. It was, however, William's need to finance his wars against Louis XIV, and the consequent financial revolution after 1688, that led to a gradual increase in the power of parliament at the expense of the monarchy.

Summarise the interpretation

Below are a sample exam question and the two extracts referred to in the question. Each extract offers an interpretation of the issue raised by the question. Summarise the interpretations offered by the extracts.

A-level: In the light of differing interpretations, how convincing do you find the view that 'the Bill of Rights brought about no fundamental alteration in the constitution' *(Extract 1)*?

To explain your answer, analyse and evaluate the material in both extracts, using your own knowledge of the issues.

AS-level: Historians have different views about how revolutionary the Glorious Revolution was. Analyse and evaluate the extracts and use your knowledge of the issues to explain your answer to the following question:

How far do you agree with the view that the Bill of Rights did not change the relationship between crown and parliament?

EXTRACT 1

Adapted from B. Coward, The Stuart Age *(1980).*

What is certain is that the members of the Convention failed to carry out the aims many of them had of putting severe limits on royal power by a Declaration of Rights. Only eleven of the twenty-eight 'heads' drawn up by the committee which reported on 2 February were included in the final version of the Declaration of Rights. It is typical of the conservative achievement of the Glorious Revolution that the Declaration retained only those 'heads' which were considered to reflect existing rights. Undoubtedly the most important of these were the declarations that the use of the suspending power, the maintenance of a standing army in peacetime, and the raising of money without the consent of parliament were illegal. Many other statements in the Declaration were so vague as to be ineffective. The Declaration left untouched most of the personal powers of the monarchy to choose its own ministers, make its own policy (especially foreign policy) and influence opinion in parliament by means of elections, placemen and the general disposition of patronage. Since the prevailing mood amongst most MPs was conservative, not surprisingly the Declaration of Rights (enacted as the Bill of Rights in December 1689) was a conservative document. It brought about no fundamental alteration in the constitution.

EXTRACT 2

Adapted from J. Miller, The Glorious Revolution *(1983).*

The Bill of Rights made it clear that the king could not legitimately keep up any permanent land forces without parliament's explicit approval: tacit connivance was no longer sufficient. The clause relating to the army was, however, the only novelty among the Bill of Rights' constitutional provisions. The remainder were largely restatements of what most people regarded as the constitution. Some were general to the point of vagueness. It was simply a series of statements of principle, often in nebulous terms. Moreover, it contained no mechanism for its own enforcement. And yet the Bill of Rights came to be seen as an outstanding constitutional document, almost on a par with Magna Carta. In explaining this apparent anomaly, we must look beyond the terms of the Bill itself. If the limitations on the monarchy which it outlined did, in fact, become established along with many others, this owed little to the amiable generalities of the Bill. The main reason must be sought in the changed relationship of crown and parliament, which had its origins not in any specifically constitutional changes but in the Revolution's financial settlement.

The impact of the Toleration Act 1689 and the end of Anglican supremacy

The Toleration Act, 1689

The Glorious Revolution changed not just the political landscape but also the religious settlement. As a Calvinist, William III was keen to secure the support of all Protestants in Britain for his war against France, and was ready to extend toleration to Catholics, as was the practice in the Netherlands. On 16 March 1689 the king asked the Commons to abandon the religious tests which kept dissenters out of public office. Keen to maintain the political supremacy of the Church of England, the predominantly Anglican parliament passed the Toleration Act in May 1689. Most dissenters:

- were exempted from penal laws if they took an oath of allegiance and declared against **transubstantiation**
- could worship freely in licensed meeting houses which had to keep their doors open
- could set up their own schools to educate their children.

However, religious toleration was not extended to Catholics, Jews or Unitarians.

The end of Anglican supremacy

The central division within Anglicanism was whether the Church should be broadened to encompass some dissenters or maintained as it was. William appointed **Latitudinarians** as bishops, for example John Tillotson, who became Archbishop of Canterbury in 1691. For Tories, such churchmen were not doing enough to prevent what they feared was the rapid growth of dissent. Tories were particularly worried by the further growth of Quakerism after the Toleration Act of 1689.

The period 1689–1701 saw a broadening of the acceptance of a range of Protestants within the Church of England. It could be argued that, in practical terms, acceptance came, slowly, not from legislation but more from the development of other ways of thinking. In particular, the increased focus on science and reason marked a shift away from the dominance of religious ideas. While after 1689 religious diversity replaced religious uniformity, religion was still central to life and also still central in shaping political attitudes.

By 1701, thanks in part to the Toleration Act, the number and the size of Protestant denominations had grown considerably. There was growing religious diversity, with Catholicism remaining strong in northern counties, while dissenting congregations grew rapidly in East Anglia. For much of the seventeenth century the Church of England could claim to be the sole religious authority in England, but by 1701 Anglican supremacy had come to an end.

Catholicism

The position of Catholics remained a source of tension from 1689 and indeed after. While it slowly became easier for Catholics to worship without interference, they remained a small religious minority, often subject to religious prejudice. Anti-Catholicism and the equation of Catholicism with the threat of Louis XIV remained a theme in English politics through to 1701 and the Act of Settlement.

The 1689 Bill of Rights excluded Catholics from the throne by removing James II and his children from the succession. It had not, however, said anything about the succession after Anne, who was next in line after William and Mary. In 1694 Mary died without any children. With the death of Anne's only child and the increasing age of William and Anne, the prospect was raised of another claim on the throne by the children of James II. As a result of the Act of Settlement:

- 57 potential Catholic heirs to the throne were excluded.
- The monarch had to be an active member of the Protestant Church of England, attending services.
- The granddaughter of James I, the Protestant Sophia of Hanover, was made next in line to the throne.

The Act of Settlement was a triumph for the Whigs. During the Exclusion Crisis of 1678–81 they had tried simply to exclude James from the succession; after 1701 exclusion would apply to any Catholic heir to the throne.

RAG – rate the extract

Below are a sample exam question and one of the extracts referred to in the question. Read the question and study Extract 1. Using three coloured pens, underline it in red, amber or green to show:

● Red: counter-arguments and counter-evidence provided by the source

● Amber: evidence that supports this interpretation

● Green: the interpretation offered by the source

In the light of differing interpretations, how convincing do you find the view that the Glorious Revolution and William's need for 'financial support' led to the end of Anglican supremacy? (Extract 1, line 8)

EXTRACT 1

Adapted from the R. Bucholz and N. Key, Early Modern England, 1485–1714 *(2004).*

The Political Nation had not revolted because they wanted a different king or constitutional settlement but because James II, enabled by his vast constitutional powers, was attacking the Protestant ascendancy. More specifically, Anglican Tories revolted because they wanted to preserve the religious status quo, in particular the special position of the Church of England as the state Church. Whig dissenters had been offered a toleration by James II, but many had refused. They had revolted against him because they felt Catholic emancipation was too high a price to pay for their own freedom. Since the leading dissenters had thus remained loyal to the Protestant ascendancy, and since dissenter goldsmith bankers and merchants provided William's government with desperately needed financial support immediately after the Revolution, Anglicans were going to have to reward them with concessions. Strengthening their argument was the further inconvenient fact that the new king was himself not an Anglican but a Dutch Calvinist – in other words, in an English context, a dissenter.

 Challenge the historian

Below are a sample exam question and one of the extracts referred to in the question. Read Extract 2, identify the interpretation offered, and use your own knowledge to provide a counter-argument, challenging the interpretation offered by the extract.

'The Toleration Act was not the final humiliation for the High Anglicans.' (Extract 2, lines 13–14) In the light of differing interpretations, how convincing do you find this view?

EXTRACT 2

Adapted from J. Miller, The Glorious Revolution *(1983).*

The Toleration Act made no ringing statements about the virtues of tolerance, but stated prosaically that 'some ease to scrupulous consciences may be an effectual means to unite their majesties' Protestant subjects in interest and affection'. It repealed none of the laws against religious nonconformity, but exempted from the penalties of those laws all who were prepared to take the oath of allegiance and make the declaration against transubstantiation and other Catholic beliefs laid down in the 1678 Test Act. This allowed Protestant Dissenters to absent themselves from Church of England services and to worship freely, provided that the meeting place was notified to the civil or ecclesiastical authorities and that the doors were locked. Dissenting clergymen could preach and minister freely, provided they took the same oath and declaration and subscribed to thirty-six of the Thirty-nine Articles. Dissenters did not become fully equal to Anglicans. The universities were still closed to them. They still had to pay tithes and church rates for the support of a church to which they did not belong. Above all they were excluded from municipal and other offices by the need to take communion in order to qualify. While such disabilities remained, Dissenters were still second-class citizens. The Toleration Act was not the final humiliation for the High Anglicans'.

The significance of the Triennial Act 1694 and the growth of parliamentary power

REVISED

The Bill of Rights of 1689 had imposed many limits on the royal prerogative. Many of the actions taken by the later Stuart kings were declared to be unlawful. In future, parliament's consent was required for the raising of taxes, the maintenance of a standing army and the suspension of some laws. William opposed these infringements on his powers of prerogative, but tolerated them in the interests of peace and harmony.

The Nine Years' War (1688–97)

William took Britain into the League of Augsburg, a coalition of European powers ranged against Louis XIV's France, and involved the country in the Nine Years' War. The war had a significant impact on domestic politics:

- William was out of the country campaigning in Europe between spring and autumn each year, and left the government of the country in the hands of his wife, Queen Mary.
- The war influenced the composition of parliament. Royal powers of patronage increased considerably as the king increased the number of MPs who also served as military officers. Many saw this process as increasing royal power over the Commons, allowing for the possible corruption of individual members, and even the creation of a 'Court Party' which would carry out the king's bidding.
- William had to summon parliament every year to gain taxes to fund the war, but he was not required to dissolve parliament at any time. This meant that there was a threat that over time parliament would become increasingly subservient to the royal will.

The Triennial Act, 1694

In 1692 the Lords agreed a Triennial Bill which would establish regular elections every three years. It was passed by the Commons but vetoed by the king. Other measures were vetoed in 1693 which, to many MPs, called to mind the anti-parliamentary stance taken by Charles II and James II.

A powerful campaign was mounted by MPs on all sides of the House of Commons for a Triennial Bill, which finally became law in 1694. It stated simply that no future parliament could last longer than three years.

Effects of the Triennial Act

- The Act removed one of the most important of the crown's prerogative powers. Before this point, the monarch had been able to dissolve a parliament which challenged the royal will, or to extend the life of one which followed the king's wishes. The Act therefore marked a substantial increase in the powers of parliament.
- Although the Act was intended to limit royal interference in the Commons, patronage and pensions were still granted to MPs ready to obey the royal will.

In the long term, frequent elections increased party rivalry and the growing divisions between the Whig and Tory parties. These reached their height in the later years of Queen Anne's reign. Anne had not produced a living heir, and on her death the Act of Settlement would be triggered, which would establish the Protestant House of Hanover on the throne. Many Tories who were still loyal to the Stuarts were determined to try and block the Hanoverian succession.

ⓘ Challenge the historian

Below are a sample exam question and one of the extracts referred to in the question. Read the extract, identify the interpretation and use your own knowledge to provide a counter-argument, challenging the interpretation offered by the extract.

In the light of differing interpretations, how convincing do you find the view that parliament had become an institution of government by 1701?

EXTRACT 1

From D.L. Smith, A History of the Modern British Isles, 1603–1707 *(1998).*

The Crown's desperate need for tax revenues transformed Parliament from an occasional event into a permanent institution of government. It is a remarkable fact that the English Parliament has met every year since 1689. This trend was reinforced by the Triennial Act of 1694, but the really binding guarantee of Parliament's continuous existence was the monarch's dependence on its taxes. The huge financial demands of war ensured that annual sessions of Parliament had become an absolute necessity. Parliament was in a position not only to withhold its consent to taxation, but also to dictate how tax revenue was spent and to scrutinise the economy: without its active cooperation, public confidence in the legitimacy of the tax system – and with it the readiness to pay such high levels of taxation – would have collapsed.

Parliament exploited this opportunity to the full. During the 1690s the principle of 'appropriation' was established, whereby parliamentary grants could only be used for the purpose for which they had been voted. The 'power of the purse' became much greater than ever before, and Parliament made increasingly frequent and ferocious use of it, not least by 'tacking' clauses redressing constitutional grievances onto revenue bills that the Crown simply could not afford to veto.

ⓘ Recommended reading

Below is a list of suggested further reading on the growth of parliamentary power in the years 1688–1701.
- C. Rose, *England in the 1690s*, Chapter 3, John Wiley (1999)
- J. Miller, *The Glorious Revolution*, pages 70–78, Longman (1997)
- D.L. Smith, *A History of the Modern British Isles, 1603–1707*, pages 306–321, Blackwell (1998)

The importance of William III's wars in the development of a financial revolution

In 1689 William III took both Britain and the Dutch Republic (where he was still the hereditary ruler) to war against France. Britain had last been involved in European conflicts during the Hundred Years' War, which ended in 1453, but the Nine Years' War was fought on a much larger scale. Over 70,000 troops were involved in the conflict, and the cost of financing the war was over £5 million per year.

In order to meet the high costs of the war many changes were made to the British financial system. The changes to the taxation system, and to the ways in which governments raised public loans, have been described by many historians as a 'financial revolution'. However, the political and constitutional effect of these developments also had long-term implications for the government of the country, and marked a profound shift in power from the monarch to parliament.

Changes in taxation

- Customs and excise duties were extended to a wider range of goods, and the rates of taxation were very high. These duties could not be avoided, and provided up to a quarter of the crown's income.
- A land tax was introduced in the early 1690s, and quickly became a permanent and lucrative source of income. The rate for the tax was set at 20 per cent of the profits which landowners made from their land. By 1700 the land tax alone accounted for half of the income raised from taxation and, like the customs and excise duties, it was very difficult to avoid.

These two measures marked a revolution in the system of taxation. They established permanent and very efficient ways of raising money which continued long after William III's wars had ended.

Changes in government borrowing

The British crown had an unenviable reputation for failing to honour its debts. In 1672 Charles II had issued the Stop of the Exchequer when he was unable to repay debts totalling £1 million. His default ruined many bankers and made it harder for Charles to raise loans for the rest of his reign.

William's ministers introduced two important innovations in order to raise money:
- In 1693 the Million Loan Act was intended to raise a loan of £1 million, and repayment was guaranteed out of income from the excise duties.
- In 1694 investors were invited to raise a loan of £1.2 million to pay for the war. In return, investors were allowed to establish the Bank of England, which provided banking services as well as raising further crown loans.

As a result of these innovative ways of raising loans, the prestige of the London money markets rose, and soon London challenged Amsterdam as a major financial centre.

The impact of the financial revolution

- The financial position of the crown improved dramatically. By 1700 around 9 per cent of the nation's wealth went towards taxation.
- There was growing confidence in the reliability of the state and its ability to repay its debts.
- The crown's ability to raise funds for the war depended on an annual vote in parliament to supply funds. As a result, parliament became a permanent feature of the system of government.

Summarise the interpretation

Below are a sample exam question and the two extracts referred to in the question. Each extract offers an interpretation of the issue raised by the question. Summarise the interpretations offered by the extracts.

In the light of differing interpretations, how convincing do you find the view that the changes in the relationship between crown and parliament in the years 1688–1701 were the result of financial rather than political change?

EXTRACT 1

Adapted from J. Miller, The Glorious Revolution (1983).

Looking at the change of ruler, the Bill of Rights, the financial settlement and the Toleration Act, there seems little that was so dramatically new as to constitute a turning-point in English history, little that could merit the epithet 'Glorious' (or indeed 'Revolution'). The significance of the change of ruler was limited and the Bill of Rights contained little that was new. Only the Toleration Act marked a clear break with what had gone before. And yet the Revolution changed English government and politics profoundly and irrevocably. One of the causes of this was undoubtedly the financial settlement.

EXTRACT 2

Adapted from M. Kishlansky, A Monarchy Transformed, Britain 1630–1714 (2010).

William's reign saw the creation of a parliamentary monarchy. While there were radical Whigs who wished to embody principles which restricted royal prerogatives in the Declaration and then the Bill of Rights, the milestones were in fact quite different. Yearly sessions of Parliament were necessitated by near-constant warfare and the fact that Parliament would only vote military supply annually. Parliament assumed responsibility for royal income through the creation of the civil list, which made the king a parliamentary dependant. Finally, Parliament established the contractual nature of royal government in the Act of Succession, which not only specified the line of descent but attempted to restrict the prerogatives of William's heirs.

RAG – rate the extract

Below are a sample exam question and one of the extracts referred to in the question. Read the question, study the extract and, using three coloured pens, underline it in red, amber or green to show:

- Red: counter-arguments and counter-evidence provided by the source
- Amber: evidence that supports this interpretation
- Green: the interpretation offered by the source

In the light of differing interpretations, how convincing do you find the view that, with the introduction of the Triennial Act, the 'year 1694 is significant' in changing the relationship between crown and parliament? (Extract 3)?

EXTRACT 3

Adapted from B. Coward, The Stuart Age (1994).

The year 1694 is significant in the history of Britain after the Glorious Revolution in more than one respect. In the developments of the constitution it saw the introduction of the principle that Parliament should in future underwrite government debts; consequently, annual parliaments were needed thereafter to maintain the monarchy's financial credit. If this was in any doubt, the Triennial Act was a further reminder that the pressure of war was forcing William to concede more of the Crown's constitutional powers than ideally he would have liked.

Exam focus (AS-level)

Below is a high-level answer to an AS-level exam-style Section C question. Read it and the comments around it.

Historians have different views about how revolutionary the Glorious Revolution was, in the years to 1701. Analyse and evaluate the extracts and use your knowledge of the issues to explain your answer to the following question.

How far do you agree with the view that as a result of the Glorious Revolution, England had become a parliamentary monarchy by 1701?

EXTRACT 1

From Edward Vallance, The Glorious Revolution: 1688 – Britain's Fight for Liberty *(2006).*

If the Revolution did not represent the advent of parliamentary 'democracy' it certainly enshrined parliamentary government. Through its increasing control over government expenditure, its power to scrutinise public accounts and later through the statutory device of the Triennial Act, Parliament became an integral, permanent institution at the heart of government. This revolution in Parliament was accompanied by a financial revolution which laid the foundations for Britain's emergence as a great power in the eighteenth century, through the creation of new institutions such as the Bank of England.

The change of monarchs ushered in cultural, as well as political, change. Many contemporaries spoke as much of a Williamite 'reformation' as 'revolution': 1688 was seen as an opportunity to return divine blessings upon the nation in terms of its salvation from popery, through a thorough reformation of public morals and manners. The popularity of this campaign remains a matter of historical debate, but it is a reminder that the Glorious Revolution did not represent the abrupt dawn of a secular age. Christian religion remained at the core of public and private life and religious controversy could be as raw and vindictive as it had been in the 1640s.

EXTRACT 2

From Jonathan Scott, England's Troubles: Seventeenth-century English political instability in European context *(2000).*

For William monarchical power was essential to war. Accordingly, the constitutional changes of 1689–1701, while securing parliaments, also recovered the military substance of English monarchy after a century of disaster. This parliamentary monarchy was the centrepiece of the newly constructed English state. It was thus in the context of this military struggle that there occurred all those constitutional alterations that amounted to the creation of a strong parliamentary monarchy. In addition to the new financial settlement, these included the Declaration of Rights; the regulation by statute of the succession; and the surrender of the sole monarchical government of Parliament's being.

Extract 1 argues that the Revolution brought about an increased role for parliament and that parliament also became a more fundamental part of government through its key influence over finance. The co-operation between monarch and parliament led to parliamentary monarchy. Extract 2 qualifies this, but also accepts that William retained a central role as monarch. One of William's primary motives for taking the throne and attempting to alter the constitution was his need for military assistance and funding to fight the Nine Years' War, suggested in Extract 2 where Scott refers to the 'military substance of English monarchy'. Overall, the evidence suggests that the monarchy did change, but in a way that was not as revolutionary as some historians suggest.

> A strong introduction that briefly explains the opinions of the two extracts and provides some contextual information.

Extract 1 argues that 1688 'certainly enshrined parliamentary government ... Parliament became an integral, permanent institution at the heart of government'. This fundamentally came about more because of the financial rather than political revolution. William's priority was to fight the French and thereby remove the threat to the Dutch Republic. The English political elite were willing to support this in return for the removal of the threat of Catholicism

> There is direct focus on Extract 1 in this paragraph, linked to contextual knowledge, with an evaluation of how far England became a parliamentary monarchy.

Quick quizzes at **www.hoddereducation.co.uk/myrevisionnotes**

by removing James II. William's war against Louis XIV also had the potential to protect Britain from European Catholicism and absolutism. William recognised that he needed the agreement of the Political Nation so that his wars could receive adequate parliamentary finance. To do this, the financial and political reforms of the Triennial Act and the creation of the Bank of England to administer a national debt in 1694 meant that parliament did, as Extract 1 argues, become a 'permanent institution at the heart of government'. The continuation of William's war further reinforced this power and regularity of parliament. It was this regular and 'integral' role for parliament through finance that was key in the development of parliamentary monarchy.

Extract 2 places stress on the importance of the financial aspects of the revolution in changing the relationship between crown and parliament and thereby creating a parliamentary monarchy. Scott argues that 'the constitutional changes of 1689–1701, while securing parliaments, also recovered the military substance of English monarchy'. For Scott in Extract 2, it 'was thus in the context of this military struggle that there occurred all those constitutional alterations that amounted to the creation of a strong parliamentary monarchy'. The need to finance the war reinforced the influence of parliament. Parliament's influence through finance can be seen in the 1673 Test Act. After 1688 this influence was taken a stage further through the sheer scale and regular need for parliamentary finance for William's wars, as Extract 2 suggests. In 1698 William's wars resulted in a national debt of nearly £17 million, due to his raising funds through long-term loans. William's willingness to formalise this power in parliament through the Triennial Act indicated the more formal shift in the balance of power between crown and parliament. It was this financial revolution, Extract 2 argues, that moved England to become more of a parliamentary monarchy.

Extract 1 argues that 1688 'did not represent the advent of parliamentary "democracy"' and it is clear that after 1688 the elite still held political power – but increasingly exercised this power through the development of parliamentary monarchy. Parliament's role developed as it was central in funding William's wars. Indeed, it could be argued that its power increased and thus created a parliamentary monarchy in which the monarch had to work much more in co-operation with parliament than before. In 1688–89 the Glorious Revolution led to significant political change in that a divine right monarch was forced from the throne and replaced by a Dutch ruler in alliance with the elite of the Political Nation, who had in effect staged a coup against the legitimate ruler. For Extract 1, the 'change of monarchs ushered in cultural, as well as political, change'. Many contemporaries spoke as much of a Williamite 'reformation' as 'revolution'. This foreign coup moved England away from a form of absolutism that had been constructed by Charles II and James II after the defeat of exclusion, and towards a parliamentary monarchy.

The 'change of monarchs' in Extract 1 was linked to a new constitutional arrangement that also allowed the development of a parliamentary monarchy. The Declaration of Rights and the new coronation oath indicated a new relationship between crown and parliament, which can be seen in the reference in Extract 1 to the changed role of parliament. Extract 2 also recognises that the Revolution, through the 'Declaration of Rights', also brought about a change in the relationship between crown and parliament. On 13 February there was a formal ceremony offering the crown to William and Mary, at which the Declaration was read out. On 11 April, at William and Mary's coronation, there was a different coronation oath from that sworn by previous monarchs, indicating the different position of the monarchs and of parliament. Rather than an oath to 'confirm to the people of England the laws and customs to them granted by the Kings of England' William and Mary swore an oath 'to govern the people of this kingdom of England, and the dominions thereunto belonging, according to the statutes in Parliament agreed on, and the laws and customs of the same'. The Political Nation represented in

This is a focused paragraph with good contextual knowledge.

There is some very good contextual knowledge here and some assessment of the extract in explaining why the changes brought about by the revolution led to parliamentary monarchy, through the consolidation of the elite's power through parliament.

parliament were able to formalise the power they had held, over the centuries, through their landholding – this is what Extract 1 regards as parliament becoming 'permanent' – and through this create a parliamentary monarchy.

Extract 1 refers to the Revolution bringing about a 'salvation from popery' and makes a link between the defeat of Catholicism and the shift from absolutism to more influence for parliament, and thus another element in the development of parliamentary monarchy. The Revolution did also bring about religious change – this could also be seen in the context of the influence of the political elite, through parliament wanting a religious settlement on their terms rather than the one dictated to them, as had been the case with James II. In shaping the religious settlement after the Revolution, in co-operation with William, parliament again illustrated the development of a parliamentary monarchy. The intervention of the Political Nation against James was, after all, religiously driven. The Political Nation moved against James because of the religious threat he posed. For them, his imposition of Catholicism meant the imposition of absolutism. The removal of Catholicism therefore also brought about an increased influence for parliament. William of Orange was a Protestant, and while he had a link to the throne through his wife, Mary, his chief attribute would be to protect the Protestant succession. The religious settlement after 1688–89 shows the power of parliament, in that they secured the church they wanted, rather than the broader church the Dutch Calvinist William would have liked. The bulk of the Political Nation were essentially conservative Anglicans and this kind of church, despite the Toleration Act, is what they preserved. The Political Nation represented in parliament kept the church as another form of their control and power, and in doing so illustrated their role in the developing parliamentary monarchy.

> The link between religion and political influence is developed from Extract 1. While there is an immediate link to the extract at the beginning of the paragraph and implied judgement at the end, there could be more focus on the extracts.

Extract 2 does, however, qualify the shift towards parliament by stressing that the monarch was still central in the developing parliamentary monarchy. While Extract 2 argues that this 'parliamentary monarchy was the centrepiece of the newly constructed English state', it was clear that it was William who was shaping policy, as his war against France was very much the central policy of this period. Parliament gained influence by supporting his policy – it could therefore be argued that the initiative lay with the monarch in the development of parliamentary monarchy.

In conclusion, both Vallance and Scott argue that parliament became more prominent as a result of the Glorious Revolution, and it is clear from the evidence that this is generally correct. The place of parliament within the constitution was enshrined through the Bill of Rights and the Triennial Act, and more regular elections would lead to a more exciting political climate. It is also clear, however, that this change only came about with the consent of William, and many of the changes he made to politics, religion and finance ultimately served to benefit his own monarchy.

This is a sound response but there is clearly room for development of use of the extracts. The candidate deploys a lot of good contextual knowledge to indicate a strong grasp of the period 1688–1701 and the development of a parliamentary monarchy, which is the focus of the question.

Maintaining focus

There is a lot of detail on the impact of the Revolution and the developing role of parliament. Go through the essay and underline every mention of the term 'parliamentary monarchy', which is the focus of the question.

Below is a sample answer to an A-level exam-style Section C question. Read it and the comments around it.

In light of differing interpretations, how convincing do you find the view that the Glorious Revolution had transformed England into a constitutional monarchy by 1701 more because it was a 'pragmatic compromise' than because of any revolutionary ideals? (Extract 1)

To explain your answer, analyse and evaluate the material in both extracts, using your own knowledge of the issues.

EXTRACT 1

From D.L. Smith, A History of the Modern British Isles, 1603–1707 (1998).

The Revolution Settlement of 1688–89 was a pragmatic compromise that sought to re-establish political stability by consciously appealing to as wide a range of opinion as possible. In general it achieved this aim very successfully and only the two extreme ends of the ideological spectrum were left alienated. On the one hand were those Tories who still regarded James as the rightful King. At the other extreme stood the commonwealthmen, or 'True Whigs', frustrated republicans who lamented the failure of the Revolution Settlement to impose limitations on the Crown. They felt that a great opportunity had been missed to change the nature of the constitution rather than just the ruler. In between, the moderate majority could live with a compromise settlement. It gained broad support by making it possible to believe different things about the events of 1688–9, especially about the extent to which James had been lawfully resisted and how far his successors were bound by a contract.

EXTRACT 2

From J. Morrill, The Nature of the English Revolution (1993).

The Sensible Revolution of 1688–89 was a conservative Revolution. It did not create damaging new rifts in the English nation. The constitutional settlement and the ecclesiastical settlements were both fudges. It was possible in 1689 for all kinds of people to continue to believe all sorts of contradictory things. Such ambiguities kept the peace in 1688. In establishing a new pattern of constitutional relationships; in creating a new context within which men and women had to make sense of spiritual and moral imperatives; in crystallizing out the two great parties; in forcing a redefinition of England's relationship to Europe and the world, thereby bringing on administrative and institutional change, the events of 1688–89 quickened and nurtured a distinctive phase in British historical development. Whether this process is called Glorious, Respectable, or just plain Sensible, it is certainly a Revolution.

Smith, in Extract 1, argues that 'The Revolution Settlement of 1688–89 was a pragmatic compromise'. Rather than a change driven by revolutionary ideals or the extremes of Tories or the Whigs, for Smith the key to the success of the revolution of 1688 was that 'the moderate majority could live with a compromise settlement'. For Smith it 'gained broad support by making it possible to believe different things about the events of 1688–89' and thus support it. There is much to support Smith's interpretation of the events of 1688–89 in that the Political Nation, both Whigs and Tories, had actively supported William of Orange's invasion to lead their political coup against James II, rather than it being a revolution driven by revolutionary ideals. The Political Nation were alienated by James II's attempts to impose Catholicism, which they believed would automatically bring absolutism in its place. They acted to prevent this rather than on the basis of any revolutionary ideals.

In their need to remove the threat that James posed, the Political Nation was willing to compromise, as Smith argues in Extract 1. Their priority was to secure Protestantism and its influence through parliament, rather than introduce any radical transformation based on

This opening paragraph immediately focuses on Extract 1 and through selecting the key elements of Smith's argument there is an illustration of a clear understanding of the extract.

Edexcel AS/A-level History Britain 1625–1701 Conflict, revolution and settlement 85

Historical interpretations: How revolutionary, in the years to 1701, was the Glorious Revolution of 1688–89?

revolutionary ideals. As William of Orange had as his priority the use of England's resources for his conflict with Louis XIV, as well as the context of his limited powers as Stadtholder of the Dutch Republic, he willingly accepted increased powers for parliament to secure his position in England. As a result of the Glorious Revolution, a Declaration of Rights, produced by a parliamentary committee of Whigs and Tories, was not made a condition of giving William the throne, but this Declaration stated that Catholics were never to inherit the crown. The Declaration was a compromise document, supporting Smith's argument in Extract 1, which was left deliberately ambiguous in terms of the constitutional implications of James' removal. In December 1689 a watered-down version of the Declaration of Rights was passed as the Bill of Rights. Revolutionary ideals therefore played a limited role in comparison with the pragmatic needs of both the English political elite and William in coming to an agreement to ensure stability. This agreement is indicated in Extract 1, when Smith references the work of Whigs and Tories together in constructing a 'pragmatic' settlement rather than a revolutionary settlement.

> This paragraph has a lot of contextual knowledge and Extract 1 is referenced directly in relation to specific examples.

In a similar vein to Smith in Extract 1, Morrill in Extract 2 sees these political changes as a 'Sensible Revolution' and also 'a conservative Revolution', in that it did not make radical change and certainly was not driven by revolutionary ideals. Morrill argues that 'the constitutional settlement and the ecclesiastical settlements were both fudges'. Like Smith in Extract 1, the stress in Extract 2 is on the co-operation within the Political Nation that brought about a constitutional monarchy. Both Whigs and Tories came to an agreed constitutional framework for the removal of James, and the Political Nation in general were willing to fund William's subsequent wars through a financial revolution that gave them even more influence through parliament.

> The candidate demonstrates an understanding of the arguments of Extracts 1 and 2 and sets this alongside some direct contextual knowledge.

There was also a change in the religious settlement as a result of the change of monarch. This change was not revolutionary, but could be argued to be more a reformation of Protestantism. Morrill, in Extract 2, references the 'ecclesiastical' settlement. In May 1689 the Toleration Act exempted dissenters from penal laws if they took an oath of allegiance and declared against transubstantiation. They still, however, could not hold public office because of the Test and Corporation Acts. This was much less tolerant to dissenters than the Calvinist William would have wanted, and was therefore a compromise with the Political Nation, who were predominantly Anglican and whose support William needed. This compromise element is why Morrill, in Extract 2, uses the term 'fudge'. Smith, in Extract 1, does not directly reference religious changes, but within the term 'Revolution Settlement' recognises the pragmatism of the agreements reached in 1688–89.

> The strong contextual knowledge in this paragraph is directly related to key phrases in Extract 2, and there is also some link to the argument in Extract 1.

William was willing to participate in a remodelling of the monarchy and state in order for the fiscal-military state to allow him to conduct global warfare against France. While change may not have been based on revolutionary ideals, the Glorious Revolution can still be regarded as bringing about revolutionary change. The political elite established a constitutional monarchy with their power more centrally located in a more powerful institution of parliament, and it resulted in the development of the financial market in London in order to finance this war. It was this compromise, more than the compromises of Whigs and Tories in removing James II that are outlined in Extract 1 and Extract 2, that was the real revolution.

> This is a rounded conclusion which has some specific contextual knowledge. It links back to the extracts.

This is a good response. It demonstrates an understanding of the extracts and integrates elements of them with good contextual knowledge. The answer has a clear structure with direct shaping to the wording of the question.

Glossary

Absolutist Monarch with unlimited powers.

Anglican Moderate Protestant member of the Church of England.

Arminianism Form of Protestantism that was a reaction to Puritanism and the desire for further reformation. Seen as the Protestants closest to Catholicism because of their emphasis on ceremony and outward forms of religion.

Arrears Money owed to the New Model Army soldiers to compensate them for pay which they had not received during the civil war.

Baptists Protestant religious group derived from Puritans, becoming more prominent after 1640 and seen as the root of many later, more radical sects.

Billeting Placement of soldiers into private houses where they would receive food and a bed.

Bishops' War Name given to Scottish Rebellion against Charles I from 1637 because of the religious nature of the opposition to Charles I.

Blasphemy Act Passed in 1650 by the Rump Parliament as a response to the development of more threatening radical religious groups like the Ranters.

Books of Orders Books sent to local government officials setting out their authority and duties in executing legislation on a range of subjects, particularly helping the poor.

Calvinists Named after the Swiss Protestant reformer John Calvin (1509–64). Calvinist doctrines were accepted by the Church of England.

Catholicism Branch of the Christian Church, headed by the Pope.

Constitution The rules by which a state is governed. At this time, there was no 'written constitution' and England was said to be governed by the 'ancient constitution', a system that had evolved over time.

Constitutional monarchy Monarchy limited through control by parliament.

Constitutional royalism Reaction by moderates worried by the development of parliamentary radicalism in the period 1640 to 1649.

Conventicle Act Act to outlaw the meeting of groups of non-conformists in the Restoration period unless they received a licence from the government.

Coup Attempt to overthrow the set order or remove key leadership figures from power. The events of 1648 and 1688 can be regarded as coups.

Court of High Commission Church court through which non-conformists could be prosecuted for non-compliance with Laudianism in the 1630s.

De facto / De jure A de jure monarch or government is the recognised legal, legitimate ruler or government. A de facto monarch or government is the one in possession of power. Many in the 1650s would still have regarded Charles II's exiled court as the de jure government.

Declaration of Indulgence Issued by Charles II and James II in an attempt to broaden religious tolerance.

Dioceses Areas under the jurisdiction of bishops.

Dissenters Post-Restoration non-conformists who did not agree with the established Church of England.

Divine right Belief that the monarch was God's representative, therefore a key justification for royal prerogative.

Dowry Payment made by a father to facilitate the marriage of his daughter.

Empiricism Scientific enquiry based on evidence.

Enclosure Farming technique of closing off open fields into smaller areas for cultivation and preventing more general common use.

Exclusion Term for the attempts to exclude or prevent James, Duke of York from succeeding to the throne when Charles II died.

Favourites Those favoured by the monarch and thereby benefiting from the access to the monarch that was key to political influence.

Fifth Monarchists Name given to the millenarians who became a more formal political and religious grouping from about 1650.

Forced loan Method of prerogative income used by Charles I in 1626.

Gentry Section of society below the aristocracy, who formed the bulk of the Political Nation, being represented in parliament and controlling local government alongside the aristocracy. There were different degrees of gentry status, all based on landed wealth.

Glorious Revolution Term used to describe William of Orange's invasion to remove James II, creating a constitutional monarchy in England.

Godly Term used by Puritans to describe themselves.

Hearth Tax Wealth tax paid on each fireplace in a building.

Huguenots French Protestants.

Humble Petition and Advice The 1657 constitution which, initially, included the offer of the crown to Oliver Cromwell.

Impeachment Means by which parliament could attempt to remove a minister of the crown.

Indemnity Insurance against prosecution. In this period, particularly applying to the concerns of the soldiers in 1647, as well as those who might be exempted from punishment at the Restoration.

Inflation Economic term for the increase in prices over a period of time.

Instrument of Government Britain's first written constitution that established Oliver Cromwell as Lord Protector in 1653.

Jesuits A religious order seen as the aggressive arm of the Catholic Church that fought to convert Protestant countries to Catholicism.

Joint stock company An association of individuals in a business with shares of stock that can be traded. Stockholders are liable for the debts of the business

Kingship Term for the offer of the crown to Oliver Cromwell.

Latitudinarians Those churchmen who were willing to accept a broad range of Protestant opinion within the Church of England.

Laudianism Term for Arminianism during the dominance of the Church of England by William Laud, from 1628 to 1640.

Major-Generals Eleven New Model Army officers appointed to rule England and Wales directly in 1655–56.

Martial law Legal authority and political control exercised by military authority.

Mercantilism Development of trade deliberately to favour exports over imports.

Militia Ordinance Parliament's establishing of its right, without royal assent, to raise armed forces in March 1642.

Millenarianism Belief in the end of the world as foretold in the Bible and specifically the Books of Daniel and Revelation, marked by the second coming of Christ and the establishment of his kingdom. This belief was common, but groups like the Fifth Monarchists believed that the end of the world was imminent.

Muggletonians Group of religious radicals that emerged from the English Revolution.

National Covenant Organisation of resistance by Scottish Presbyterians to Charles I.

Non-conformists Term for those who were outside the Church of England after 1660.

Patriarchal Male-dominated society with the monarch seen as the father of his people. This concept reinforced the power of the monarch and fathers over their families but with it came the duty to provide for and protect those in their care.

Political Independents Term for a minority group in parliament, linked to the New Model Army in the build-up to the execution of Charles I in 1649.

Political Nation The political class; members of society who influence how a country is run. In early modern Britain, it included the landowning aristocracy and gentry, as well as other wealthy individuals sometimes referred to as 'the elite'.

Political Presbyterians Term for a majority group in parliament, linked to the Scottish Presbyterians in the build-up to the execution of Charles I in 1649.

Prerogative Power of the crown, in theory derived from God as divine right. From divine right the powers of the crown were referred to as the prerogative.

Presbyterian Those who supported a church with a government of equal presbyters, or elders, often appointed by the congregation, rather than other systems such as episcopacy (bishops).

Protectorate Term for the rule of Oliver Cromwell as Lord Protector, as established by the written constitution, the Instrument of Government.

Puritans Radical Protestants who saw themselves as 'godly', sometimes referred to as 'the hotter sort of Protestant'. They sought a further reformation of the English church to remove the vestiges of Catholicism that remained from the Reformation.

Quakers Radical religious group that emerged in the 1650s and grew rapidly.

Ranters Radical religious group that emerged in 1649–50 and became the subject of scandalous reports in the press.

Recusant Term used to describe those who refused to attend the services of the Church of England.

Reformation   Process by which England became a Protestant nation under Tudor monarchs in the sixteenth century.

Regicide   Execution of the monarch, or those that arranged it. The regicides were those 59 men who signed the death warrant of Charles I, although the act of regicide was supported by others, notably in the New Model Army and those of more radical religious views.

Scottish Kirk   The church in Scotland.

Secret Treaty of Dover   Agreement of 1670 by which Charles II would receive funds from his cousin Louis XIV in exchange for keeping parliament from sitting.

Ship Money   A prerogative form of income that a monarch could levy on coastal towns to provide emergency funds in time of conflict or threat, in order to defend coastal regions and equip the fleet.

Subsidy   The main form of parliamentary tax.

Test Act   Act introduced in 1673 to prevent Catholics from holding any public office.

Tithes   Tax of one-tenth of an individual's income that was used to support the Church of England.

Tonnage and poundage   The right to raise revenue for the whole of the monarch's reign from imports and exports.

Tory   Term for those moderate Anglicans who supported the crown in the period from 1678.

Transubstantiation   The Catholic belief that, during Mass, the bread and wine are literally transformed into the body and blood of Christ.

Vestments   Elaborate robes that ministers of the Church of England were supposed to wear when conducting services.

Visitations   Method of reporting through which bishops checked the imposition of Laudianism in their areas of influence in the 1630s.

Whig   Term for political group that emerged around the desire for exclusion.

Key figures

Francis Bacon (1561–1626)   Philosopher, scientist and statesman. He became Lord Chancellor under James I but was impeached in 1621. He is known for developing the scientific method, which placed emphasis on the importance of experimentation in scientific understanding.

Henry Bennet, 1st Earl of Arlington (1618–85)   Catholic who advised Charles II during exile. He supported the Dutch War in the 1660s and was created Lord Arlington in 1665. He opposed Clarendon and was the main force behind the Secret Treaty of Dover. The Test Act forced his chief ally, Clifford, to resign. He lost influence with the rise of Danby.

Thomas Clifford, 1st Baron Clifford of Chudleigh (1630–73)   Catholic, became a Privy Councillor in 1666, helped to negotiate the Secret Treaty of Dover. He advised Charles to declare the Stop of the Exchequer and publish the Declaration of Indulgence. He was made Lord Treasurer in 1672 and opposed the Test Act of 1673, resigning from office.

Anthony Ashley Cooper, Earl of Shaftesbury (1621–83)   Supported parliament in the civil war but openly supported the Restoration in 1660. An opponent of Clarendon, Cooper came to power in the Restoration as part of the Cabal and was made the Earl of Shaftesbury. He opposed the Duke of York's succession and went into exile in 1682.

Oliver Cromwell (1599–1658)   Came to believe through his experience on the battlefield that God had judged Charles I. Through his command of the New Model Army in 1653 Cromwell was made Lord Protector, head of state, until his death.

Thomas Fairfax (1612–71)   Appointed commander-in-chief of the newly created New Model Army in 1645. With the politicisation of the army, Fairfax found himself increasingly sidelined and resigned in 1650.

Thomas Harrison (1606–60)   One of the most radical officers in the army, he was clear in his judgement of Charles I as 'that man of blood'. He commanded the troops that brought the king from Windsor to his trial in London. Attending nearly all the sessions of the trial, Harrison was a prominent regicide. At the Restoration he was the first regicide to be executed.

Thomas Hobbes (1588–1679)   During the years 1640 to 1652 Hobbes was based in Paris and it was here that he wrote his key work, *Leviathan* (1651). The final section of this work was a justification of submission to England's new republican regime.

Edward Hyde, 1st Earl of Clarendon (1609–74)   Leading Constitutional Royalist to 1642, advisor to Charles Stuart during his exile and at the Restoration became Charles II's chief minister until he was forced into exile in 1667.

Henry Ireton (1611–51)   Responsible for most of the political statements of the army from the Solemn Engagement, the Heads of the Proposals to the Remonstrance that called for the execution of Charles I. He played a leading role in the politics that led to the regicide.

John Lambert (1619–84)   New Model Army officer who worked alongside Henry Ireton in producing the Heads of Proposals in 1647. After Ireton's death he became the leading army theoretician who, through his written constitution, the Instrument of Government, made Cromwell Lord Protector.

William Laud (1573–1645)   Leading Arminian, appointed Archbishop of Canterbury by Charles I in 1633. Executed by parliament in 1645.

John Lilburne (c1614–57)   Puritan who attacked the Laudian bishops in print and helped distribute the works of similar-minded Puritans. When he left the army in 1645 he returned to writing pamphlets and became a leading figure in the movement known as the Levellers, which called for social and political reform.

John Locke (1632–1704)   Philosopher who published his most famous work, *Two Treatises of Government*, in 1689. His work became more widely read in the eighteenth century, especially in light of the American Revolution.

Louis XIV (1638–1715)   Inherited the throne at the age of four, but did not take sole power until 1661. Under Louis XIV the French monarchy reached the pinnacle of its power, with Louis being the model of absolutism. Known as the 'Sun King', Louis had a palace at Versailles which was a visible symbol of his power. More real was the expansion of French power through war. In a series of seven wars between 1661 and 1715 Louis extended French control across what is essentially France today. In contrast, Charles II's two wars against the Dutch highlighted the weaknesses of England as a European power and when he signed an alliance with Louis in 1670 he became, in effect, a client of the French crown.

John Maitland, Duke of Lauderdale (1616–82)   Presbyterian who supported the Covenant but promoted engagement and support for Charles II. He was captured at Worcester and imprisoned until 1660. He was appointed Secretary of State for Scotland at the Restoration, persecuted Conventicles in Scotland, and resigned in 1680.

George Monck (1608–70)   Cromwell persuaded this ex-royalist to command the New Model Army in Scotland in the 1650s. He began to establish links with Charles II and his intervention into English politics in 1659–60 was crucial in bringing about the Restoration. After the Restoration Charles II made Monck the Duke of Albemarle.

Richard Montagu (1577–1641)   Arminian cleric who was at the centre of controversy at the start of Charles I's reign due to his publication of anti-Calvinist tracts. Charles' support and promotion of Montagu escalated the dispute into a more serious constitutional question.

Thomas Osborne, Earl of Danby (1632–1712)   Emerged as Charles II's chief minister after the Cabal, when he was appointed Lord Treasurer in 1673 and created Earl of Danby in 1674. He arranged the marriage of Mary, the Duke of York's daughter, to William of Orange. He came under suspicion for being a supporter of absolutism and was removed from influence by Charles II.

John Pym (1584–1643)   Highly visible in the parliaments of the 1620s and pre-eminent in the Commons of 1640 to 1642, to the extent that from the autumn of 1641 he was referred to as 'King Pym'.

George Villiers, Duke of Buckingham (1592–1628)   Became the favourite of Charles I. As Lord High Admiral, Buckingham was seen as responsible for foreign policy failures. Attacked by parliament, he was defended by Charles. He was assassinated in 1628.

William of Orange (1650–1702)   Stadtholder of the Dutch Republic. William was married to Mary, daughter of James, Duke of York, and thereby had a link to the English throne. As a result of his struggle against Louis XIV, William saw England as a possible extra resource to overcome the strength of the French monarch. The invitation from the English elite for him to invade in 1688 saw him become William III. During his reign the state was remodelled as a constitutional monarchy.

Timeline

1625	Charles I crowned king; Failure of Buckingham's expedition to Cadiz	1649	Charles I tried and executed; Diggers establish a commune in Surrey
1626	Forced loan levied	1651	Navigation Act
1627	Failure of Buckingham's expedition to La Rochelle; Five Knights' case	1653	Cromwell expels the Rump; The Nominated Assembly; Cromwell made Lord Protector
1628	Petition of Right; Assassination of Buckingham	1658	Oliver Cromwell dies
1629	Peace with France	1659	Richard Cromwell removed from office
1630	Peace with Spain	1660	Charles II issues the Declaration of Breda; Restoration
1633	Charles crowned in Scotland; William Laud made Archbishop of Canterbury	1662	Act of Uniformity
1635	Ship Money levied on whole country	1667	Removal of Clarendon
1637	Outbreak of the Scottish Rebellion	1670	Secret Treaty of Dover
1639	First Bishops' War	1672	Charles II forced to issue the Stop of the Exchequer
1640	Parliament called	1673	Test Act
1641	Irish Rebellion; Grand Remonstrance passed	1677	William of Orange marries James' daughter, Mary
1642	Attempted arrest of five MPs; Charles I leaves London; Militia Ordinance passed; Outbreak of civil war in England	1678	Popish Plot; Exclusion Crisis
1645	Creation of the New Model Army	1685	Death of Charles II; James II becomes king
1646	Defeat of Charles and royalists in First Civil War; Newcastle Propositions sent by parliament to the king	1688	James flees London; William enters London
1647	Scots hand Charles I over to parliament; Politicisation of the New Model Army; Heads of Proposals presented to Charles	1689	William and Mary offered the crown; Toleration Act
		1694	Bank of England founded; Triennial Act
1648	Parliament breaks off negotiations with Charles; Outbreak of the Second Civil War; Pride's Purge	1701	Act of Settlement

Mark schemes

AO1 mark scheme

- **Analytical focus**
- **Accurate detail**
- **Supported judgement**
- Argument and structure

AS Marks		A-level Marks
1–4	**Level 1** • Simplistic, limited focus • Limited detail, limited accuracy • No judgement or asserted judgement • Limited organisation, no argument	1–3
5–10	**Level 2** • Descriptive, implicit focus • Limited detail, mostly accurate • Judgement with limited support • Basic organisation, limited argument	4–7
11–16	**Level 3** • Some analysis, clear focus (may be descriptive in places) • Some detail, mostly accurate • Judgement with some support, based on implicit criteria • Some organisation, the argument is broadly clear	8–12
17–20	**Level 4** • Clear analysis, clear focus (may be uneven) • Sufficient detail, mostly accurate • Judgement with some support, based on valid criteria • Generally well organised, logical argument (may lack precision)	13–16
	Level 5 • Sustained analysis, clear focus • Sufficient accurate detail, fully answers the question • Judgement with full support, based on valid criteria (considers relative significance) • Well organised, logical argument communicated with precision	17–20

A03 mark scheme

- Interpretation and analysis of the extracts
- **Knowledge of issues related to the debate**
- Evaluation of the interpretations

AS Marks		A-level Marks
1–4	**Level 1** • Limited comprehension of the extracts demonstrated through selecting material • Some relevant knowledge, with limited links to the extracts • Judgement has little or no support	1–3
5–10	**Level 2** • Some understanding of the extracts demonstrated by describing some of their relevant points • Relevant knowledge added to expand on details in the extracts • Judgement relates to the general issue rather than the specific view in the question, with limited support	4–7
11–16	**Level 3** • Understanding of the extracts demonstrated through selecting and explaining some of their key points • Relevant knowledge of the debate links to or expands some of the views given in the extracts • Judgement relates to some key points made by the extracts, with some support	8–12
17–20	**Level 4** • Understanding of the extracts demonstrated through analysis of their interpretations, and a comparison of the extracts • Relevant knowledge of the debate integrated with issues raised by the extracts. Most of the relevant aspects of the debate are discussed – although some may lack depth • Judgement relates to the interpretations of the extracts and is supported by a discussion of the evidence and interpretations of the extracts	13–16
	Level 5 • Interpretation of the extracts demonstrated through a confident and discriminating analysis of their interpretations, clearly understanding the basis of both their arguments • Relevant knowledge of the debate integrated in a discussion of the evidence and arguments presented by the extracts. • Judgement relates to the interpretations of the extracts and is supported by a sustained evaluative argument regarding the evidence and interpretations of the extracts.	17–20

Answers

Page 7, Spot the mistake

Religion was an important issue in undermining the relationship between Charles I and the parliament in the years 1625 to 1637. From 1625 Charles sought to impose Arminianism as his favoured approach to the Church of England. In doing so he alienated the majority of the Political Nation. In 1626 Charles responded to parliamentary calls for the impeachment of Montagu by provocatively promoting the Arminian cleric to be his royal chaplain. In 1626 Charles sent his favourite, Buckingham, to make his support for Arminianism clear at the religious conference held at York House. In 1628 he promoted William Laud to Bishop of London, again signalling his support for Arminian clerics. In all of these things he did not seek any compromise but believed he had the right, as Supreme Governor of the Church, to do what he wanted in religious policy. After 1629 Charles continued to impose Arminianism through Laud whom he made Archbishop of Canterbury in 1633.

Page 9, Complete the paragraph

Some of Charles' measures included forest fines and the selling of monopolies. All of these raised his income and thereby improved his financial position. The most significant form of fiscal feudalism that improved Charles' financial position was Ship Money. Through this, from 1634 to 1639, Charles received £200,000 a year. That this was the equivalent of approximately three parliamentary subsidies indicates that not only did Charles improve his financial position, he also achieved his other financial aim of doing so without having to call a parliament.

Page 9, Delete as applicable

Charles I's imposition of Laudianism undermined his government to a **fair** extent. For example, the 'beauty of holiness', which involved the introduction and enforcement of the use of more visual forms of religion, was unpopular with Puritans. This involved the use of vestments and music as part of services. Laudianism was enforced through the use of visitations and church courts. Charles I's imposition did not undermine his government as the visual aspects of Laudianism were **moderately** successful **by 1640 in invigorating the church without provoking significant opposition. Thus while Puritans may have disliked the imposition of Laudianism they were a minority, whereas the majority accepted the changes passively.**

Page 15, Identify the concept

How accurate is it to say that the development of opposition to Charles I's religion since 1625 was the main reason for his eventual execution in 1649? CHANGE

How accurate is it to say that the execution of Charles I was more the result of the politicisation of the New Model Army than the alienation of parliament? SIGNIFICANCE

To what degree was the position of Charles I stronger in 1646 than it was in 1625? CHANGE

How accurate is it to say that the king's execution in 1649 was a response to the political actions rather than the religious policies of Charles I since 1637? SIMILARITY

Page 21, Develop the detail

In 1660 Charles II's priority was to stay on the throne. He faced a number of serious immediate problems in 1660, specifically what to do with the New Model Army and the interlinked structural problems that hampered all early modern monarchs: finance, the constitution and religion. Charles dealt with all pragmatically to secure his immediate position on the throne but in doing so did not resolve these fundamental structural problems of the early modern state. In taking such a pragmatic approach to his Restoration Charles II avoided alienating the Political Nation in parliament, on which all monarchs knew they had to rely, but in doing so he failed to reform and the issues of finance, religion and the constitution remained problems throughout his, and James II's kingship. The Glorious Revolution of 1688-89 brought their resolution through a change in the relationship between Crown and Political Nation through the development of a more constitutional monarchy.

Page 25, Complete the paragraph

James succeeded, however, in alienating the political elite through his attempts to give Catholics not only more freedoms but also real power. In doing so he acted in an increasingly absolute way. It was, however, the birth of a son to James in June 1688, and thereby the prospect of a Catholic succession, that made the Political Nation stage a coup, with the aid of a foreign invasion by William of Orange.

Page 29, Developing an argument

Charles' drive to impose Laudianism during his Personal Rule provoked more opposition than the actual nature of Laudianism itself. The majority of the Protestant nation were anti-Catholic and saw Laudianism as a form of Catholicism. If, however, they had the freedom to worship in their own style the majority wished to be loyal to the crown and would have still felt part of a Church of England, even if Laudianism was prominent in it. It was, however, Charles' determination that all conformed to Laudianism that appeared to give them no choice but to oppose his imposition of Laudianism.

Page 31, Complete the paragraph

In doing so it meant that they did not have to oppose directly the authority of those in power to secure the forms of worship they wanted, as the Presbyterians had to in 1637, and this reduced religious tensions.

Page 33, Simple essay style

Introduction:

Puritanism was a threat to Charles I in the years 1625 to 1638 because most Puritans wanted a more reformed Church of England along more Puritan lines than Charles was willing to enact as Supreme Governor. Furthermore, his imposition of Arminianism alienated them, as they believed he was moving the church more in the direction of Catholicism, even further from what they wanted. Nevertheless, most Puritans were not a serious threat to Charles as they were a minority group and only a small number of them were prepared to take direct action against the authority of Charles.

Key points:
- Nature of Puritanism – anti-Catholic and viewed Laudianism as Catholic; minority of the population and unpopular with many; vocal and organised minority, including influential members of the Political Nation.
- Puritan emigration – most went to the Dutch Republic or New England; approximately 15,000 left during the 1630s to set up 'godly' Puritan communities away from Laudianism; companies organising emigration, such as the Providence Island Company, provided a framework for opposition to the regime.
- Impact of the Scottish Rebellion – Presbyterian reaction to the imposition of Laudianism; National Covenant movement had links to leading Puritan opponents of Charles I in England such as John Pym; provided an example and encouragement of opposition to Puritans in England.
- Puritan opposition after 1637 – Prynne, Burton and Bastwick; John Lilburne; popular iconoclasm.

Conclusion:

Puritan emigration during the 1630s removed a lot of the potential threat of the group to Charles' authority. It was only after the example of the Scottish Rebellion and Charles' failure to crush it that Puritans in England were able to act more directly against Charles and thereby became a more serious threat to him.

Page 35, Develop the detail

In 1625 Charles I became king of England and king of Scotland but he did not visit Scotland for a formal coronation until 1633. This indicated to the Scots where his priorities were, as king of England rather than as their king of Scotland. Charles further compounded this during 1633 by making public his intention to remodel religion in Scotland. **The Scots' experience of Charles in 1633 confirmed the Scots' fears that he had little sympathy with their traditions or understood their ruling elite. He reinforced to them that, despite being born in Scotland, he was an English king first and foremost. For the Presbyterian Scottish elite Charles' imposition of the Laudian Prayer Book in July 1637 left them no other option but direct opposition to the rule of Charles I.**

Page 37, Support your judgement

While the first judgement could be generally seen as valid, the greater differentiation in the second judgement between the approaches of both monarchs gives a more accurate picture. James II moved from an initial policy of stating he would work with the Political Nation to maintain the Church of England, as it was increasingly looking to change the religious settlement in favour of Catholics and dissenters. In doing so, he eventually provoked a religious revolution against him by the Political Nation.

Page 39, Simple essay style

Introduction:

Anti-Catholicism was a constant theme of the seventeenth century. The English had a long tradition of anti-Catholicism. After 1660 they were concerned about the policies of Charles and the growing threat of a resurgent France under the Catholic Louis XIV. Anti-Catholicism became more prominent, however, after 1678 because of the threat of the next monarch being a Catholic. When James did come to the throne, the coup against James was based on the Political Nation being against his aggressive promotion of Catholicism.

Key points:
- Anti-Catholicism – historical context; Catholicism seen as linked to absolutism; concern at nature of Charles II's court, its prominent individuals and baroque style.
- Louis XIV – established himself as the most powerful European monarch after 1660, the 'Sun King'; cousin of both Charles II and James II; developed links with both English monarchs, e.g. Secret Treaty of Dover 1670.
- Exclusion Crisis – attempt to exclude James, Duke of York, from the throne from 1678 because he was a Catholic; popular participation in anti-Catholic protests; exclusion defeated by Political Nation questioning the necessity of it, suggesting they were willing to contemplate a short-lived Catholic reign by James.

- Glorious Revolution – coup by the Political Nation in reaction to the promotion of Catholicism by James II; trigger for revolution was the birth of James' son and the prospect of ongoing Catholic rule; William of Orange's invasion triggered by fear of Louis XIV.

Conclusion:

Anti-Catholicism was a constant theme of the years 1660 to 1688. The Glorious Revolution was, however, the high point of anti-Catholicism after 1660 in that it ended in the removal of the legitimate monarch and his replacement by a foreign Protestant ruler, William of Orange, with the co-operation of the Political Nation.

Page 61, Spot the mistake

There was no agricultural revolution in the seventeenth century. Progress was made predominantly not so much because of new techniques but because of the impact of new ideas and crops. The role of finance and the reorganisation of farmland also had a significant impact. The population stagnated after 1650 and the progress in farming techniques enabled the population to be fed even more efficiently. Poverty and starvation were unheard of by 1700.

Page 63, Simple essay style

Introduction:

Refugees coming to England in the years 1625 to 1688 did have an impact on economic development. Most refugees came to escape religious persecution and brought with them significant skills that had a social and economic impact in the areas in which they settled at different times across the period 1625 to 1688.

Key points:
- Nature of immigration – French and Flemish Huguenots; skilled artisans; immigration across the period but had peaks, e.g. Revocation of the Edict of Nantes.

- Social impact – immigration predominantly to East Anglia and London; link to Puritanism in these areas; link between social, religious and economic development.
- Economic impact – introduction of new, rather than revolutionary techniques; new draperies in East Anglia linked to immigration; increase in quality goods for developing consumer society post-1660.
- Extent of impact through the period – impact greater before 1650 in terms of development of new draperies but post-1660 in terms of development of quality goods.

Conclusion:

Refugees did have an impact on the economic development of England in the years 1625 to 1688. The development of the new draperies was significantly shaped by the new techniques and ideas of Protestant refugees. This had a significant economic impact on the areas where they settled, for example, Norwich. This impact was part of wider changes in the structure and direction of the economy of England as it increasingly replaced the Dutch Republic as the global trading power.

Page 67, Complete the paragraph

Overall, by 1688 the Navigation Acts had a significant impact in stimulating the development of English exports as they acted as a means to protect and promote the shipping of goods in English ships. Many of the goods brought in English ships to England were then in turn shipped on as an export, and by 1688 England was well on the way to becoming the dominant global trading nation.